The Food of
BHARAT

For my son and daughter

A CHEF'S JOURNEY THROUGH
INDIA'S RICH CULINARY HISTORY

The Food of
BHARAT

RECIPES FROM THE VEDIC ERA
TO THE MODERN DAY

Helly Raichura

Food photography Jana Langhorst
Location photography Brett Cole

Hardie Grant

BOOKS

Timeline

At first there was ...

Adi Parashakti

The divine feminine energy from which we were all created, to whom I bow down for her blessing. Adi Parashakti is the supreme Mother Goddess in Hinduism.

Brahma, Vishnu, Mahesh: the Creator, the Preserver, the Destroyer

In Hindu belief, Brahma creates the universe, Vishnu preserves it and Mahesh (Shiv) destroys it in an eternal cycle.

Bhagwan Ram

Bhagwan Ram is believed to be the seventh avatar of Vishnu. He is worshipped by Hindus in temples across India. There are many events celebrating his life, one of the most notable being Diwali, which celebrates the return of the god to his home after battle and exile. The ancient Indian epic *Ramayan* mentions berries, fruits and foods being eaten during this time.

Krishna

Shree Krishna is believed to be the eighth avatar of Vishnu. He is worshipped by Hindus across the country for his teachings, his role in the epic *Mahābhārat*, and his narration of the holy text *Bhagavad Gita*. Milk, ghee, butter and dairy products are much talked about as favourites of Krishna.

The Stone Age

Ended c. 3500 BCE

Humans are hunter-gatherers, and later settle around bodies of water to farm and grow food. The people of this period hunt wild animals to cook on open fires, and gather wild fruits, vegetables and fungi.

Indus Valley Civilisation

c. 3300–1300 BCE

People establish advanced ancient cities, such as Harappa and Mohenjo-daro, farm, store grains, look after animals for milk and meat, establish trade routes, and develop technology and knowledge. Trade with Africa, especially Egypt, brings grains, fruits and vegetables from faraway lands to the subcontinent.

The Vedic period

c. 1500–500 BCE

Vedic civilisation places a high value on knowledge, and the recording of knowledge, societal norms and customs. The science of Ayurveda is born, and food preparation, purpose and properties are recorded in great detail.

Dynasties rise in Magadha and the south

c. 500 BCE–500 CE

Diverse powerful dynasties rise across the subcontinent, and the advancement of trade by land and sea routes brings peace and prosperity. Traders and migrants bring foods and techniques from faraway lands, enriching the cuisine. This time marks the beginning of India as a melting pot. The spice trade peaks with spices exported and imported in great quantities. Many new spices and ingredients are incorporated into the cuisine.

The Mughal era

1526–1800

The Mughals introduce new butchery and cooking techniques, such as smoking and preserving. They introduce and cultivate fruits from central Asia and lead lavish lifestyles. Perfumed spices are used prominently in meat and rice dishes, and bread is leavened.

The colonial era

1858–1947

Carrots, cauliflowers, potatoes, tomatoes and chillies are introduced by the Portuguese and British, and later take over the palates of Indians. They become staples in every Indian household.

The present day

Today, the evolution continues. The origins, history, traditions and inventions of India's culinary past are recognised, reclaimed and honoured, so that they can be preserved and carried forward into the next chapter of the subcontinent.

Introduction

I come from a family that has always been obsessed with food and produce. Living in Ahmedabad in the west of India, we were fortunate enough to have access to abundant local produce, as well as produce from the other 27 geographically and culturally diverse states of India. Much like other families across the country, our culinary repertoire revolved around seasonal fruits and vegetables, and spices and grains.

Around November, Diwali signals the beginning of the Hindu New Year for my family and many Indians. This time also marks the end of autumn and the beginning of celebrations. During Diwali, there is joy in the air, and families visit each other with boxes of sweets, fried snacks, fireworks and envelopes filled with cash for the children. It was my favourite time of the year when I was young for many reasons. Baa (my grandmother) would source the freshest, softest and greenest lila chana (fresh Bengal gram) to make halwa from, and during the Diwali holidays my cousin and I would head to the nearby lake to pick seasonal water chestnuts.

During winter, eating chyawanprash, a jam made from amla (a native berry high in vitamin C) and several Ayurvedic herbs, was a must, and varieties of rice were stored for the entire year. In February, late-winter varieties of eggplant (aubergine) started popping up, and we devoured fresh pigeon pea kachoris (a deep-fried, stuffed snack) and added finely diced rat-tail radish to raita.

In spring, Mummy used to make my favourite vegetable dish, pointed gourd with yoghurt, and taro leaves were coated with besan (chickpea flour) batter and steamed to make patra, while phalsa (another native berry) was turned into cordial. Summer was dominated by mangoes, and the entire family would gather to make fresh mango ice cream in a wooden ice-cream churner. We would break slabs of ice by hand and layer them with salt, while everyone took turns to churn. During this time, we would also begin to store grains and spices for the entire year.

At the centre of sourcing all this beautiful produce was my fiya (paternal aunt) who either grew it herself or took us to farms to pick our own. My fiya was very particular about eating and serving skilfully preserved produce. When I entered commercial kitchens, using tweezers or incorporating flower extracts into dishes was not new to me. Growing up, I saw my baa take melon seeds out of their shells with tweezers and use rooh gulab attar (rose extract fragrances), which she would source from a trusted supplier in Mathura. My family's cooking techniques and food philosophy were clear, and perhaps ahead of their time: source your own produce, follow seasonality, preserve and ferment skilfully, consume a balanced diet, and make everything from scratch. Growing up with these guiding principles has always fuelled my curiosity and passion for cooking. My mummy would also experiment with cooking dishes from other regions of India for dinners. South Indian food was always our favourite, as we were strictly vegetarian, though Rajasthani, Punjabi, Bihari, Goan and many more regional dishes were featured on Mummy's dinner menu.

Years later in Australia while dining at fine diner Lûmé, which was then run by Shaun Quade, I was intrigued by what was on my plate. The passion that it took to form the dish was obvious, the produce was native but foreign to me, and the processes were driven by unique skills and Shaun's creative bursts. For me, this moment brought back the memory of a kitchen on a different side of the world, one where a similar passion reigned, but in a different style: my home.

I had always wanted to study culinary arts and work in kitchens, but when I was younger, office jobs were considered to be more reputable, and I was easily influenced. I pursued a business degree and spent the first 10 years of my professional life working in an office. I learned the ins and outs of how a business works, and how to live the Australian way of life. In those early days, my karma bhumi (the land where I worked) only felt like my place of work, not the place where I really lived and, after years, I yearned for that connection again. I had been working in corporations for too long, and I wanted to do something driven not by profit but for the love of process, passion and my values. I was drawn to the kitchen, and I wanted to be surrounded by its secrecy and familiarity.

So, I took up a couple of small stints at restaurants, first at Lûmé and then at fellow fine diner Gaggan. It changed the course of my life. I had felt like I wasn't myself for years, but finding myself in the kitchen, with its similar-minded people and maddening working hours, woke me from my slumber. I found a renewed energy, and once I got addicted to the adrenaline of restaurant service, desk jobs quickly became dull, and I was pulled towards starting Enter Via Laundry in Melbourne.

I ran Enter Via Laundry from my home kitchen for ten guests a night, and they literally entered via my laundry, hence the restaurant's name. In the initial days I was still trying to discover my own style of cooking. I cooked puff pastries with truffles, orange dumplings with carotene extracted from carrots, made pumpkin (squash) and yuzu ice cream, experimenting far and wide. Then, one day, I made my favourite dish, Khandavi (page 204), and by the end of service I knew that regional Indian cooking was going to be my focus.

Like many cooks, I wanted to cook food I was brought up eating, but more so, I wanted to cook food that I had yet to discover. I wanted to use native produce from my adopted home, Australia, and I wanted to know what was in season here just as my fiya had known what was in season back in our hometown in India. By this time, I had begun to connect with Melbourne, and soon we were flooded with people wanting to come and dine with us. Our waitlist spanned a year and it felt like half the city wanted to come and try my food.

Finally, I had embarked on a lifelong journey to cook, explore and discover food from my heritage. There was and is so much to learn about the culinary heritage of India, and I hope to spend my lifetime being its student. Since the early days of Enter Via Laundry in 2018, I have been researching regional Indian cuisine, discovering that to truly understand a cuisine it is important to first understand the country and its civilisation, history and evolution.

Food is a constant necessity, though how we cook changes with shifts in cultural development, population, economic conditions, technology, the environment and more. I felt an acute need to understand this evolution in Indian civilisation, and how the food had grown and evolved alongside it. I wanted to restore and build upon our understanding of Indian cuisine, eliminate long-standing stereotypes, and ignite a sense of pride in my children for their heritage, which is so ancient and versatile.

I decided to call this book *The Food of Bharat* as Bharat is the oldest-known name of the subcontinent we now call India. This book is about the evolution of Indian food, and I have divided it into five chapters. We start with the food philosophy of the earliest-known civilisations of Bharat – the Indus Valley Civilisation and the Aryans – followed by the influential trade and migration era during the Gupta age, also referred to as the Golden Era of India, when migrants and traders shaped the cuisine by adapting existing dishes with local ingredients. We then move on to the Mughal invasion, which introduced exotic new techniques and ingredients to Indian cuisine; the British and European colonial era; and, finally, modern Indian cuisine and recipes from my kitchen.

As India's history and geographical map evolved, so did its cuisine. This book is the story of my food, a compilation of the discoveries I've made from my travels in India, and a tribute to the evolution of Bhartiya Bhojan: the food of Bharat.

PRE-VEDIC AND POST-VEDIC ERA

To understand a cuisine, it is important to start with the history of the land and go back in time to discover where it started. Like a person's childhood shapes their adulthood, a land's past underpins its present. Indian cuisine reflects not only the history of India as the region we see on the map today, but of the whole Indian subcontinent which has hosted myriad dynamic and complex civilisations, tribes and cultures, all interacting and merging with each other to create the diverse contemporary Indian cuisine we know today.

My journey to discover the origins of present-day Indian dishes started in the Old Books market on College Street, Kolkata, where I began my research on prehistoric India by collecting manuscripts and books. However, my early research barely touched on food, and instead was concerned with communities, culture, politics, economy and religion. Soon, I discovered that these were the very forces that shaped the evolution of food on the subcontinent. I was curious to understand the very first foods of the land – its fruits, vegetables, animals and grains, and how they were processed, prepared and eaten.

Examining these ancient civilisations and their eating habits led me to discover one of the most significant eras in Indian history, the Vedic era. This period shaped the social structure of India, and food consumption was informed by major scriptures and religions and their strict guidelines on diets for their followers.

In the beginning, nomadic Stone Age communities traversed the land to gather food. People only settled down in the Neolithic era, when they established social structures and began to cultivate land, harvest crops and domesticate cows, goats and sheep for meat and milk, securing a steady supply of food. With food security came housing, relationships, groups, and civil structures and urban living. Evidence of these early communities has been found in Punjab, where the seven rivers converge, as well as Bihar, Orissa and Nasik. Composed of modern-day Pakistan, Bangladesh, Nepal, Bhutan, Sri Lanka and even Afghanistan, the Indian subcontinent has always proved to be fertile ground for human civilisations. Scholars estimate that human activity in the region dates back to hundreds of thousands of years BCE in

Soon Valley Punjab, Gujarat, Rajasthan, Meghalaya, Pakistan and Tamil Nadu. Many of the details of the pre-Vedic era of India are still a mystery to us.

Following the Stone Age, the most prevalent pre-Vedic civilisation on the subcontinent was the Indus Valley or Harappan civilisation, dating back to 3300–1300 BCE, with sophisticated, well-formed cities. The Harappans raised cows and used cow milk. They grew grains such as barley, peas, millet and pulses. Bones excavated from this region indicate they ate beef, mutton, turtles, small Indian alligators and fish. Large granaries that stored grains for the year were also discovered. Copper and earthenware pots have been excavated from archaeological sites dating back to this era.

In the south, Brahmagiri in Karnataka and Nagarjunakonda in Andhra Pradesh show similar evidence that food crops, like finger millet, pearl millet, sorghum and mung, were cultivated. There is mention of vegetables, like yams, sweet potatoes, eggplants (aubergines) and bitter gourd; fruits, like banana, coconut, jackfruit, pomegranate, wood apple and mangoes; and spices, including turmeric, cloves, cardamom, tamarind and mustard, in ancient literature from this time.

The emergence of the Indo-Aryans in the subcontinent around 1500 BCE heralded the beginning of the Vedic era. When the Aryans prevailed, they formed communities around the rivers in the northern parts of the subcontinent, enforcing adherence to the lifestyle set out by the Vedas. The Vedas are ancient texts that cover fundamental knowledge relating to the underlying cause of, function of, and personal response to existence. ('Veda' translates to 'knowledge'.) There are four Vedas: chronologically, the Rigveda, Yajurveda, Samaveda and Atharvaveda (which includes Ayurveda).

In ancient India the boundaries between schools of science, philosophy, astrology, medicine, law, economy and mathematics were fluid. Knowledge was acquired and imparted holistically, and religion was a medium through which this knowledge was shared to common people in the form of stories, events, poems, metaphors, rituals, practices and traditions. Food was also consumed with a holistic approach, and nourishment, taste,

medicine, mood, environment, personal health, occupation, age, sex and religion were all considered.

Ayurveda, a subsection of Atharvaveda, is a science that describes the path to a prolonged, healthy life. Health is a prerequisite to achieving anything in life, and preventive and curative disease management are fundamental components in this science. In fact, Ayurveda is regarded as one of the oldest medical practices, and food sits at its centre.

Ayurveda provided a detailed set of dos and don'ts around food, as well as remedies and recommendations. It was recommended that a stress-free environment and a pleasant mood were as necessary for appropriate digestion as the quality and nature of the food. Certain food combinations were suggested, while others were avoided, to ensure proper digestion and assimilation of nutrients. For example, rice and other grains like wheat or millet could be eaten with vegetables, and milk products like cheese, butter, yoghurt and buttermilk, but fresh milk was not to be combined with cooked or boiled vegetables. Spicy, bitter and pungent foods were also not to be combined with milk. This is why my mother still rolls her eyes when I add garlic to béchamel! Water wasn't recommended immediately before or after having a meal, as it was believed to slow the digestion process. It was necessary for food to be in season for consumption, and for grains to be soaked for hours before cooking or fermenting.

Ayurveda emphasises the digestive system's crucial role in overall well-being. Each of six tastes imparts unique energy in the body, and incorporating all of them into a meal ensures a diverse energetic profile. In Ayurveda, moderation is essential as excess can lead to imbalance.

Sweetness: revered in Ayurveda for its nourishing qualities; promotes longevity, strength and healthy body fluids

Sourness: enhances the appetite, stimulates saliva production, aids digestion, and awakens thoughts and emotions

Saltiness: supports digestion and tissue cleansing

Bitterness: the coolest taste; naturally detoxifies and purifies the body by eliminating waste

Pungency: the hottest taste; aids digestion, increases appetite, cleanses tissue and improves blood circulation

Astringency: cool, firm and dry, with anti-inflammatory properties

While the Aryans were expanding into the north of the Deccan Plateau, southern India was forming a history that was independent from the North (until later, when the South began to acquire Aryan influence). Ancient Sangam literature sheds light on the food habits of the region and talks about a variety of millets and rice, masoor and mung, that were discovered. Rice, which was boiled, fried and even puffed, was eaten with tamarind, ghee, milk, vegetables and meat. Meat was devoured in the South before the influence of the Aryans, with buffalo, boar, beef, iguana, rabbit, fish and other game birds eaten with black pepper, ginger and turmeric.

Early civilisation also flourished in the eastern region of India in the states now famously called the Seven Sisters: Nagaland, Manipur, Meghalaya, Tripura, Arunachal Pradesh, Assam and Mizoram. In Meghalaya, Neolithic remains have been found at Garo villages, and the ancient text *Yogini Tantra* mentions the use of pork with the soft roots of the banana tree, as well as wild fern, which is still a delicacy in Assam.

While civilisations of the Vedic era were initially open and liberal, providing education to all genders, as time went by, they began to disadvantage the lower castes and women, and growing

discontentment with the social hierarchy caused an eruption of new religions and philosophies to spring forth, some of which were Buddhism, Jainism, Ajivika, Bhagavatism and Shaivism. Recipes began to emerge that were not divided based on caste, but rather aimed to aid in increasing mental and physical stability. Gautama Buddha taught moderation – nothing was good in excess – and the prescribed diet was intended to bring balance and harmony, hence meat, garlic and onions, which were considered aphrodisiacs, were eliminated.

Jainism preached non-violence and penance, and according to Jain texts, abstaining from the pleasures of the senses and dwelling in consciousness was upavasa (fasting), which they considered important for the purification of the body and soul. Due to its focus on refraining from harming living creatures, the diet prescribed by Jainism was not only vegetarian but excluded even root vegetables, like potato, garlic and onions, to prevent harming insects and microorganisms. Jain cuisine is still widely upheld and prevalent in India in Jain communities, with even local

airlines offering Jain meal options. Achieving a balanced body and mind through diet is an eternal practice, and the ways in which we attempt to achieve this in the present day are often similar to what our ancestors did.

Bhagavatism, which is also called Vaishnavism, flourished alongside Jainism and Buddhism, with the focus on Krishna worship. In Krishna worship, bhakti (devotion) replaced sacrificial offerings. I grew up with this religion, and practised devotion to Krishna from an early age. My baa used to practise a Marjadi Dharam, where, aside from vegetarianism and the exclusion of onion and garlic, she also chose not to eat any foods that were not offered to her Lala (God), and nor did she eat any processed foods, hence she made everything from scratch.

In Naroda, a city in Gujarat, my in-laws serve a temple that is 110 years old. Many offerings are made to God during the day-long worship, with the temple kitchen being at the heart of it. Several old recipes have remained unchanged, with seasonal vegetables being favoured and a heavy use of bottle gourd seasoned with ginger, turmeric, cumin, black pepper and ghee. Sweets heavily feature milk and nuts, and are decorated with finesse to please the deity. Cows are worshipped and in return they provide fresh milk daily. Different religions form their own unique food habits, and diverse ways of preparing and eating food can be observed across India.

Many of the recipes in this chapter are contemporary versions of recipes mentioned in ancient literature from across India; culinary traditions that have been carried forward to the modern day; recipes from temples that have operated in the same way for centuries, giving us a glimpse into kitchens of the past; and recipes from unfolding research into ancient times on the subcontinent.

Ghee

Clarified fermented butter

Makes 150–200 g (5½–7 oz)

Ghee is essential to Indian cooking – technically, culturally, religiously, even emotionally! It is fatty on the tongue and has a nutty flavour. Often you will find ghee poured over a dish in excess to express love and generosity. We are obsessed with it, and for good reason. Besides being utterly delicious, ghee holds a sacred status in Ayurveda. 'Ayur' means 'alive', and 'ved' means 'knowledge'. The ancient scripts of India make reference to Ayurveda, prescribing practices to balance the body to enable it to perform at its best. Ghee was and still is consumed as part of an Ayurvedic practice, as well as being used in religious ceremonies by offering it to fire. Many grandmothers will suggest ghee as a single solution to multiple ailments, from dry skin to sleeplessness. Back in the day, most households had cows to look after, so cream to make ghee was plentiful. They followed strict guidelines about what to feed the cows, how to milk them and how much of that milk should be fed to the calf first. Cows were sacred, and their mistreatment was prevented by religious rules designed to pay respect to the mammals who nourished us with their milk.

500 ml (17 fl oz/2 cups) thick cream (double/heavy), or full-cream (whole) milk skin from unhomogenised milk

Utensils

Patili or heavy-based pot

This recipe is very practical for a household that uses fresh milk on a daily basis. Back home to this day, fresh milk isn't stored for more than a day even in the fridge. Milk is boiled every morning and left to cool to be used for different applications. Once cool, a layer of cream forms on top of the milk, and this is collected every day and stored in the fridge.

After a couple of weeks, you would accumulate, ideally, about 500 ml (17 fl oz/2 cups) fermented cream to make ghee.

Place the cream in a patili or heavy-based pot over a medium heat. Warm gently for 30–40 minutes until the milk solids and fat separate. Try not to stir too much – just often enough to prevent the cream catching on the base of the pot. The ghee will float to the surface and the milk solids will turn from white to dark brown.

Take the pot off the heat. Once the ghee has cooled to room temperature, carefully strain the ghee through a muslin (cheesecloth) or fine-mesh sieve.

Store the ghee at room temperature in a sealed container or sterilised glass jar for up to 1 month. (You can sterilise a jar by placing it in a saucepan of boiling water for 30 seconds, then leaving it to air-dry.) The pat – the milk solids that caramelise in the process of making ghee – can be eaten with a little sugar sprinkled on top as a dessert.

I love ghee on a hot rotla (see page 62).

Ghee, the cheat's version

Makes 350 g (12½ oz)

Heat the butter in a patili or heavy-based pot over a medium heat until it reaches 140°C (285°F) on a cooking thermometer. Remove any impurities that rise to the surface with a slotted spoon. No pat is produced in this version.

Take the ghee off the heat, let it cool, then strain and store in an airtight container or sterilised glass jar (see method, page 38) at room temperature for up to 1 month.

500 g (1 lb 2 oz/2 cups) unsalted butter

Utensils
Patili or heavy-based pot
Slotted spoon

Takra

Probiotic yoghurt drink

Takra is called chaas in Gujarati, with some variations being called lassi. It is a creamy, slightly tart and refreshing drink. Takra is, essentially, a probiotic-rich drink which is referred to as Amrit (the divine nectar) in Ayurveda. It is a digestive that promotes gut health and immunity, with Ayurveda claiming that drinking takra daily resolves and prevents the recurrence of diseases, and has a flow-on effect to improving intelligence and mental clarity through its effect on the gut. Takra is supposed to be taken after lunch every day. The proportion of fat added to takra is decided based on a person's gut health – full fat for a healthy gut, medium fat for a less healthy gut and no fat for someone whose gut is healing. Here, we will be making takra with a medium amount of fat which would be appropriate for the majority.

500 ml (17 fl oz/2 cups) unhomogenised full-cream (whole) milk

25–50 g (1–1¾ oz) plain yoghurt, at room temperature

½ teaspoon toasted cumin seeds, coarsely crushed

Utensils

1 litre (34 fl oz/4 cup) metal or glass jar

Mathani (wooden churner) or a hand-held blender

Bring the milk to the boil in a pot over a high heat, then turn off the heat and allow the milk to cool down. In cooler climates, allow the milk to cool to 60°C (140°F), and in warmer climates, bring it to 40°C (105°F).

Add 25 g (1 oz) of the yoghurt to the warm milk if you're in a warmer climate, and 50 g (1¾ oz) in a cooler climate. Mix gently.

Cover with a lid and leave to ferment in a warm place for 12 hours. Once fermented, the yoghurt will keep in a covered container in the fridge for up to 4 days.

To make takra, take 120 g (4½ oz) yoghurt with the fat that forms as a skin on top of the set yoghurt, and place it in the jar.

Top with 400 ml (13½ fl oz) water and add sea salt to taste.

Scatter the toasted cumin seeds on top and blend with a mathani or a hand-held blender to break up the lumps and make it frothy. Serve at room temperature.

Matulai

Pomegranate stir-fried with curry leaf

Another interesting dish mentioned in the first-century Tamil poem *Perumpānārruppatai* is pomegranate and curry leaf. It is fresh and tart, but fragrant too with the addition of curry leaf and pepper. The great food historian K T Achaya mentions a poem that describes food offered to a wandering minstrel by all six occupational classes that existed during the time of Aryan influence in south India. There is mention of grains and millet boiled in milk, fish and rice, red rice and iguana, fowl, and sweetmeats, and there is mention of food offered by Brahmins, which is fine rice with mango pickle and pomegranate cooked with ghee and curry leaves.

30 g (1 oz) Ghee (page 38)
1 large curry leaf sprig, leaves stripped
500 g (1 lb 2 oz) pomegranate seeds
½ teaspoon ground black pepper

Utensils
Kadhai or heavy-based wok

Heat the ghee in a kadhai or heavy-based wok over a medium heat. Add the curry leaves and, once they stop popping, add the pomegranate seeds and mix well.

Add the pepper and some salt and mix well. Cook the pomegranate over a high heat for 1 minute.

Take off the heat and serve as a side or, as mentioned in the ancient poem, with rice and mango pickle.

Baingan sabji

Braised eggplant with spices and ginger

Serves 2–3

In 2010, archaeologists Arunima Kashyap and Steve Weber used starch analysis to trace a handi (cooking vessel) made of earthenware which was excavated from Farmana in the Ghaggar-Hakra valley near modern-day Delhi. Through this analysis, they claimed they discovered the 'proto', or 'original' curry, which I would really call a sabji, or braised vegetable. Braised eggplant (aubergine) is prepared in most Indian regions, and each has its own unique take on the dish. The eggplants in this recipe are silky, and the spices are mild but flavourful. When I had just given birth to my son, I was given a special diet by my mother. It is believed that new mothers should eat certain foods when breastfeeding to aid a newborn's digestion. What appeared most frequently on the menu was eggplant sabji with ginger, turmeric and black pepper cooked in ghee.

Crush the ginger and garlic to a smooth paste with a mortar and pestle.

Heat the sesame oil in a kadhai or heavy-based wok over a medium heat. Fry the crushed ginger and garlic till slightly brown, then add the eggplant.

Increase the heat to high, stir to coat the eggplant in the oil, then add the turmeric and salt to taste, and mix well. Cook for 1 minute.

Mix the eggplant one more time, scraping the bottom of the pot. Lower the heat to medium, cover the kadhai and cook for 7 minutes, stirring periodically, or until the eggplant is soft.

For a modern-day take, add some finely chopped coriander and some freshly ground black pepper to garnish. Serve with Bajra rotla (page 62) or rice.

20 g (¾ oz) piece fresh ginger, peeled and roughly chopped

10 g (¼ oz) garlic cloves, peeled

30 ml (1 fl oz) sesame oil, or Ghee (page 38)

800 g (1 lb 12 oz) eggplant (aubergine), destemmed and cut into bite-sized cubes

1 teaspoon ground turmeric

finely chopped coriander (cilantro) and freshly ground black pepper, to garnish (optional)

Utensils

Kadhai or heavy-based wok

Note

Always use fresh eggplant, as older eggplant doesn't cook as well and out-of-season eggplant creates an unpleasant tingling sensation on the tip of the tongue.

Dudhi nu shak

Braised bottle gourd with spices

In my religion of Pushtimarg, dudhi (bottle gourd), which is also called lauki and sorakkai, holds great importance. At Naroda Bethak temple in Ahmedabad, where my in-laws stay, there are strict guidelines about what can and cannot be made and offered to God, as well as how it is prepared and who prepares it. Only select Brahmins are allowed in the kitchen, and the kitchen that uses milk in preparations is separate from the kitchen that does not. Any red-coloured ingredients are not allowed, and any aphrodisiac foods like onion and garlic are prohibited. Food is strictly vegetarian. Dudhi has been used in India since 2000 BCE and is considered a cooling food that maintains balance in the gut, as it is easily digested and rich in nutrients. Here I will be sharing a simple recipe for what is cooked as an offering to the gods. This shak is light and aromatic with cumin and ginger.

Heat the ghee in a kadhai or heavy-based wok over a high heat until hot.

Add the cumin seeds and cook until they become darker brown and start popping, then add the asafoetida followed by the grated ginger and cook for 10–15 seconds.

Now add the cubed dudhi and stir until well coated in the ghee. Cook for another 20 seconds.

Sprinkle the turmeric over and season with salt to taste, and mix again.

Continue cooking over a high heat for 1 minute, then lower the heat to medium–low and cover the pot with a lid. Cook for 8 minutes, or until the dudhi is soft and starts releasing its own liquid.

Add the jaggery, mix well, and then take the pot off the heat. Serve with Bajra rotla (page 62).

Serves 2

30 g (1 oz) Ghee (page 38)
1 teaspoon cumin seeds
3 pinches of asafoetida
25 g (1 oz) piece fresh ginger, grated
800 g (1 lb 12 oz) thin dudhi (bottle gourd), peeled and cut into small cubes
1 teaspoon ground turmeric
1 teaspoon grated jaggery

Utensils
Kadhai or heavy-based wok

Vagharela mung

Stir-fried whole green mung beans

Mung beans, being a native product of India, have been in our diet for a long time, and are high in dietary fibre and protein. This recipe is made in many regions in India, and mung is especially significant for the Jain community in India's west. Jainism, which has rigorous dietary restrictions that support its teachings of nonviolence and no harm towards insects and even microorganisms, teaches its followers to be pure vegetarians with the further restriction of not eating tubers, onion, garlic and, at times, even green vegetables or fresh coriander (cilantro). During Chauvihar fasting, where no food or water is consumed after sunset until the following day, mung is eaten at Navkarsi, the first meal after sunrise. Mung beans are nutty in flavour and herbaceous with the addition of ground cumin and ground coriander.

250 g (9 oz) whole green mung beans
30 ml (1 fl oz) vegetable oil
2 pinches of asafoetida
1 teaspoon ground turmeric
1 teaspoon ground coriander
½ teaspoon ground cumin
1 teaspoon freshly ground black pepper

Utensils
Patili or heavy-based pot
Kadhai or heavy-based wok

In a patili or heavy-based pot, cook the mung beans in 1.5 litres (51 fl oz/6 cups) boiling salted water for 15 minutes, or until the beans are soft but not mushy. Drain, then set aside.

Now in a kadhai or heavy-based wok, heat the oil over a medium heat. Once hot, add the asafoetida followed by the turmeric, coriander and cumin. Give it a quick stir, then immediately add the cooked mung beans and mix well. Increase the heat to high and cook for 5 minutes.

Mix again, scraping the bottom of the kadhai, then check and adjust the seasoning and continue to cook for another 5 minutes.

Add the pepper and mix well, then take it off the heat.

This can be eaten by itself as breakfast, or it can be served as part of a larger meal with roti and rice.

Appam

Fermented rice bread

Serves 8

South Indian literature from the third century CE mentions several foods made with rice, of which one is appam, a type of pancake eaten with milk. By this period, the south Indians had already developed several methods of processing and storing rice grain. Rice was aged for 2–3 years for a better texture and aroma, then it was parboiled and dried. This recipe uses equal parts parboiled rice and raw rice to get the desired texture. Urad dal was a later addition, but it is now a must in appam. Fenugreek seeds are added to aid in the natural fermentation process. Back in the day, the batter was likely ground by stone, as it continues to be in households throughout India. Crushing instead of cutting the rice produces a better fermentation and fluffier appams.

400 g (14 oz) uncooked white medium-grain rice

400 g (14 oz) parboiled white medium-grain rice

100 g (3½ oz) urad dal

1 teaspoon fenugreek seeds

2 g (⅟₁₆ oz) jaggery

100 ml (3½ fl oz) coconut milk

40 g (1½ oz) coconut oil

Utensils

Stone grinder or blender

Appa chatti or deep, heavy-based small wok

Tavetha or wooden spatula

In a big bowl, wash the two varieties of rice and the dal separately three times, then soak each for at least 5 hours.

Grind the rice grains separately with a little water in a stone grinder or blender to a slightly coarse batter.

Grind the urad dal to a fine paste with up to 175 ml (6 fl oz) water.

Mix all three batters together. Your mixture should be the consistency of cake batter – add more water if needed. Add the fenugreek seeds and mix well.

Cover with a plate, leaving room for the batter to expand as it ferments. Leave in a warm place to ferment for 12 hours.

Once fluffy, add some salt to taste, the jaggery and the coconut milk, and mix well. The consistency of the batter should now be thinner than a cake batter but thicker than a pouring consistency, so adjust with a little water if the batter is too thick.

Heat an appa chatti or a deep wok with two handles over a medium heat and add ⅛ teaspoon of the coconut oil. Tilt it to grease the wok, then wipe the wok out with a paper towel.

Scoop 100 g (3½ oz/¼ cup) of the batter at a time and add it to the appa chatti or wok, and swirl to coat the sides. Then place the lid on top.

Cook for about 4 minutes over a medium–low heat until the sides are light brown and the centre is bubbly and cooked. With a tavetha or wooden spatula, carefully scrape the side to detach the appam from the wok and gently remove the cooked appam to a plate. Repeat until all the mixture has been used.

Serve with Ghee (page 38) and milk, sambar (see page 53), chutney or pickles.

Temple sambar

Pumpkin with lentils, coconut and spices

Sambar, the ever-popular south Indian staple often made with lentils, is a soupy spicy dish eaten with rice. Sambar has been mentioned in ancient Sangam literature, with a parallel theory suggesting that its origins may even point to the Maratha Empire. Here, we are cooking a fragrant, tangy and fresh pumpkin (squash) sambar. Pumpkins, which are native to North America, somehow travelled to India too, and a must for any sambar is the inclusion of fresh tamarind pulp which brings a delightful warmth and depth to the dish.

Start by preparing the masala. To a dry kadhai or heavy-based wok, add the coriander and cumin seeds, chana dal, urad dal, fenugreek seeds and peppercorns and toast lightly over a low heat.

Place them on a sil batta or in a spice grinder with the curry leaves, coconut, oil and tamarind pulp and crush to a smooth paste. Add some water if needed to adjust the consistency.

Now to a patili or heavy-based pot, add the pumpkin, turmeric, tamarind pulp, jaggery and a good pinch of salt. Add 1.2 litres (41 fl oz) water and the masala paste and mix well.

Place the pot over a medium heat and simmer the soup for 5–7 minutes until the pumpkin is soft but not mushy. Add a little more water if necessary to achieve a pouring consistency, keeping in mind that the dals will thicken the mixture.

Now we are ready for tadka. This process needs to be quick and hence all the tadka ingredients need to be ready in advance. Heat the ghee in a vaghariyu or small pot over a high heat until hot. Now add the mustard seeds, followed by the curry leaves and asafoetida. Once the mustard seeds stop popping, add the tadka to the sambar.

Return the sambar to a high heat and let it come to the boil. Give it a taste, and if you want it sourer, add more tamarind and adjust the seasoning with salt, then mix well. Take it off the heat and serve with rice or Appam (page 51).

850 g (1 lb 14 oz) pumpkin (squash), peeled, seeds removed, cut into bite-sized pieces

1 teaspoon ground turmeric

5 g (⅛ oz) tamarind pulp (available at Indian grocers), plus extra if needed

35 g (1¼ oz) jaggery

Masala

3 tablespoons coriander seeds

3 g (¹⁄₁₀ oz) cumin seeds

10 g (¼ oz) chana dal (split chickpeas)

10 g (¼ oz) urad dal

3 g (¹⁄₁₀ oz) fenugreek seeds

8 g (¼ oz) whole black peppercorns

15 g (½ oz) curry leaves

75 g (2¾ oz) shredded fresh coconut

15 ml (½ fl oz) vegetable oil

15 g (½ oz) tamarind pulp

Tadka

30 g (1 oz) Ghee (page 38)

4 g (⅛ oz) mustard seeds

½ small curry leaf sprig, leaves stripped

2 pinches of asafoetida

Utensils

Kadhai or heavy-based wok

Sil batta or spice grinder

Patili or heavy-based pot

Vaghariyu or small pot

Pakhala bhata

Fermented rice with fried eggplant and fish

This recipe is a breakfast staple from Orissa, an eastern state of India, that has been eaten for generations. This simple dish is made from left-over rice soaked in water, and eaten the next day with chopped ginger, fried eggplant (aubergine) and fried fish. The soaking of the rice ferments it, which increases the amount of nutrients and probiotics in the rice. These days, charred tomatoes, green chillies and garlic are added, all of which were introduced much later to the region.

Put the cooked rice in an earthen bowl with 200 ml (7 fl oz) room-temperature water. Cover, and let it soak overnight.

The next day, add a pinch of salt and the ginger, mix and set aside.

To cook the eggplants, first coat them with most of the turmeric, reserving a little for the fish, and a pinch of salt. Set aside for 10 minutes.

Heat enough mustard oil for deep-frying in a kadhai or heavy-based wok over a medium–high heat to 180°C (360°F). Deep-fry the eggplants until cooked, about 2 minutes. Keep the oil hot to fry the fish.

Coat the fish with the remaining turmeric and some salt.

Deep-fry the fish until the flesh is cooked and the skin is crisp, about 3 minutes.

Add the fermented rice to a serving bowl and serve with the fried fish and eggplant.

200 g (7 oz) cooked white short-grain rice, at room temperature

10 g (¼ oz) piece fresh ginger, peeled and julienned

1 baby eggplant (aubergine), halved

2 g (¹⁄₁₆ oz) ground turmeric

mustard oil, for deep-frying

2 small gutted whole fish of your choice

Utensils
Earthen bowl
Kadhai or heavy-based wok

Malpua

Fried reduced milk in sugar syrup

Malpua is one of the most ancient foods in Indian cuisine, mentioned even in Vedic literature from 5000 years ago. Malpua is a rich, moreish dessert, oozing with sugar syrup and flavoured with fragrant spices. It is still made as prasad (holy food offering to a deity) in many temples, though the recipes now have evolved to include baking powder or bicarbonate of soda (baking soda) and more dairy to enhance its richness. Malpuas come in several varieties, and it is likely that the original iterations were made by frying a batter made from millet or barley flour and then sweetened with honey, sugarcane syrup, dates, or bananas, as these were the popular ingredients available at the time. Spices like cardamom, saffron, fennel and even pepper are added to some recipes, with each region making its own version. Here, I am sharing a simple recipe that uses some basic pantry staples and fragrant spices.

500 g (1 lb 2 oz/2 cups) Ghee (page 38), for frying

split green cardamom pods, slivered almonds or slivered pistachios, to garnish (optional)

Batter
1 litre (34 fl oz/4 cups) full-cream (whole) milk, plus 75 ml (2½ fl oz) extra
50 g (1¾ oz/⅓ cup) plain (all-purpose) flour
pinch of baking powder

Sugar syrup
115 g (4 oz/½ cup) caster (superfine) sugar
pinch of saffron threads
seeds of 2 green cardamom pods

Utensils
Patili or heavy-based pot
Tavetha or wooden spatula

To make the batter, add 2 tablespoons water to a patili or heavy-based pot and tilt to coat. Add the milk and bring it to the boil over a medium heat.

Reduce the heat to medium–low and cook until it has reduced to about 250 ml (8½ fl oz/1 cup), stirring periodically. The milk should form laces, or milk skin. Remove from the heat.

This is called basundi, or rabdi, and it's the base for several Indian desserts.

Add the flour, baking powder and extra milk, stir, then let it sit for 15 minutes.

To make the sugar syrup, add the sugar and 60 ml (2 fl oz/¼ cup) water to a small saucepan and melt over a medium heat for 6 minutes. Turn off the heat. Crush the saffron threads and cardamom seeds with 1 teaspoon water with a mortar and pestle to make a paste, then add it to the sugar syrup.

Heat the ghee in a large saucepan to 150°C (300°F) on a cooking thermometer. Working a ladle at a time, ladle the batter carefully into the hot ghee. Cook until the top is no longer visibly wet and the side is starting to brown. Flip the malpua with the help of a tavetha or wooden spatula and cook on the other side until golden brown.

Remove from the pan and immediately drop the malpua in the sugar syrup to soak for a minute, then remove to a serving plate. Repeat with the rest of the batter. You can cook multiple malpuas at the same time depending on the size of your saucepan.

To serve, place on a serving plate, drizzle with more sugar syrup and garnish with the cardamom pods or slivered nuts, if using.

Payasam

Sweetened rice cooked in milk

Serves 4

Payasam is a sweet and creamy dessert with a soft bite of rice and flavoured with cardamom. Payesh, kheer and payasam are some names for a sweet preparation of rice, milk and jaggery. This dish is considered holy, and is often fed to babies weaning off their mother's milk. It is also used as a sacred offering to gods in temples. Payasam receives mentions in the *Mahābhārat* and other ancient texts, where stories are narrated around it, and since the sugars used in ancient times were palm sugar or jaggery – refined sugars were not introduced to Indian diets until much later – I have chosen to use jaggery for this recipe.

15 g (½ oz) Ghee (page 38)

100 g (3½ oz) Sona Masoori rice, soaked for 1 hour then drained

1.1 litres (37 fl oz) full-cream (whole) milk

120 g (4½ oz) jaggery

seeds from 2 green cardamom pods, crushed to a powder

30 g (1 oz) slivered almonds

10 g (¼ oz) raisins

fresh rose petals, to garnish

Utensils
Kadhai or heavy-based wok

Heat the ghee in a kadhai or heavy-based wok over a medium heat. Once it has melted, add the drained rice and turn gently to coat each grain with the ghee. Toast for 4 minutes, ensuring you don't brown the rice.

Now add the milk and continue to stir over a medium heat.

Continuously scrape the bottom of the pot and keep stirring to avoid the mixture catching. Cook until the rice is soft but not disintegrated, about 10–15 minutes, then add the jaggery, mix and cook for another 5 minutes.

Take it off the heat and add the powdered cardamom seeds, slivered almonds and raisins, mixing well.

Serve warm or leave in the fridge to cool before garnishing with fresh rose petals.

Bajra rotla

Pearl millet flatbread

Serves 2

Bajra, or pearl millet, and several other millet varieties are believed to have come to India from Africa about 3000 BCE. Millet is a gluten-free grain used in several applications. Where I grew up in Gujarat, pearl millet is widely used for making rotla, a flatbread that is eaten with ghee, butter or braised vegetables. This gluten-free bread is not the easiest flatbread to shape; women often make these breads by shaping them with their hands and a little water before cooking them on an earthenware flat pan called a lodhi. Shaping the dough into round, thin discs by hand takes years of practice. Here, I have created a version that can be simply rolled out with a rolling pin.

300 g (10½ oz/2 cups) bajri atta (pearl millet flour), plus extra for dusting

185 ml (6 fl oz/¾ cup) warm water

10–20 g (¼–¾ oz) Ghee (page 38)

Utensils

Lodhi or flat pan

Mix the bajra atta with a good pinch of salt. Add 125 ml (4 fl oz/½ cup) of the warm water and start kneading the dough. Add the remaining water as needed to create a soft dough. Knead for at least 10 minutes.

Create 60 g (2 oz) balls of dough and cover with a cloth.

Using a rolling pin, roll the balls into discs about 15–18 cm (6–7 in) in diameter, dusting the benchtop with flour as needed.

Heat a lodhi or flat pan over a low heat and drop the rotla in. Cook on one side for about 30 seconds, then flip, increase the heat to medium and cook the other side until a few light-brown spots appear on the rotla.

Now take the rotla, thread it onto a long fork and hold it over an open fire, or the gas flame of your stovetop, with the less cooked side facing the heat. The rotla should puff up in 3–4 seconds.

Take off the heat and spread with ½ teaspoon ghee, then set aside. Repeat with the remaining dough.

Serve warm with Baingan sabji (page 45) or eat with milk for breakfast.

Vada

Lentil fritters

Serves 4

Another dish mentioned in ancient literature is Vada. These fritters come in several forms, but all use lentils – washed, soaked and ground with spices, then lightly fermented and deep-fried and eaten with chutney. To date, Indian society loves vada for breakfast, as an accompaniment to lunch, or as a snack for afternoon tea. From street vendors to homes and temples, vada is still popular for its flavour and versatility.

Wash the urad dal a couple of times in cold running water, then soak in a bowl of cold water for at least 3 hours.

Drain the dal and blitz in a blender or grind with a wet stone grinder into an almost-smooth paste. Add water if needed to adjust the consistency, but remember that the batter needs to be thick.

Place in a bowl and 'whisk' the batter with your fingers for 5–6 minutes until light and airy.

Add salt to taste, the black pepper, ginger and rice flour. Mix well and set aside for 2 hours to ferment a little.

To make the coconut peanut chutney, heat the vegetable oil in a frying pan over a medium–low heat and roast the peanuts for 8 minutes, then remove.

Add the peanuts to a blender with the coconut, fresh turmeric, jaggery, tamarind paste and a pinch of salt. Add a little water and blend to a smooth paste. Transfer the paste to a bowl.

Heat the ghee in a vaghariyu or small pot over a medium heat. Once the ghee is hot, add the mustard seeds and, once they stop popping, add the curry leaves and asafoetida, then after a couple of seconds, pour over the chutney. Mix well, check the seasoning and set aside.

To test that the batter is fermented, drop a little into a glass of water. If it floats, enough air has been incorporated. If it doesn't, whisk again with your fingers until the batter is fluffy enough that it floats when tested in the water.

Heat enough oil for deep-frying in a large saucepan until it reaches 150°C (300°F) on a cooking thermometer. Drop about 30 g (1 oz) of the batter into the oil with a spoon and deep-fry until golden on both sides, about 8–10 minutes.

If you prefer, you can shape your fritters into a doughnut shape before frying. Dip your hands in water, take 30 g (1 oz) of batter and form a ball, then flatten into a thick disc. Gently press a hole through the middle to make a doughnut shape, then drop the vada into the hot oil and deep-fry until golden on both sides.

Serve with the coconut peanut chutney.

400 g (14 oz) urad dal
15 g (½ oz) crushed black peppercorns
40 g (1½ oz) piece fresh ginger, grated
60 g (2 oz/⅓ cup) rice flour
vegetable oil, for deep-frying

Coconut peanut chutney
½ tablespoon vegetable oil
30 g (1 oz) peanuts, shelled
200 g (7 oz) freshly grated coconut
10 g (¼ oz) fresh turmeric, peeled
5 g (⅛ oz) jaggery
10 g (¼ oz) tamarind paste
1 tablespoon Ghee (page 38)
1 teaspoon mustard seeds
1 curry leaf sprig, leaves stripped
2 pinches of asafoetida

Utensils
Vaghariyu or small pot

TRADE
AND
MIGRATION

Kashmiri kahwa
Warm saffron and spice tea 80

Bhinda par ida
Eggs on okra 83

Potol dolma
Fish-stuffed pointed gourd 84

Patrani machi
Fish marinated with coriander and
coconut and steamed in banana leaf 88

Kozhi porichathu
Chicken with onion and turmeric 91

Tharavu roast
Roast duck with gravy 92

Kavuni arisi idli
Steamed fermented black rice batter 97

Chilli pork
Pork with chillies and soy sauce 98

Pathiri
Rice flour flatbread 100

Modaka
Pastry stuffed with coconut and jaggery 101

Several dynasties rose, fell, flourished and withered in the next chapter of the Indian subcontinent. During the sixth century BCE, Magadha in the north-east emerged as one of the principal kingdoms, ruled by dynasties such as Haryanka, Shaishunaga, Nanda and later Maurya. Magadha traded with north, east and south India through mastery of the rivers and sea.

Later, in the third century BCE, the Asoka Empire, which stretched from Hindu Kush to Mysore, promoted the manufacture of salt, muslin (cheesecloth), silk, dye, iron, gold and copper. Routes across land greatly improved during this time, connecting the north-west to the north and central India, which linked the ancient cities of Sravasti, Pratisthana and Taxila. Bhrigukachchha (now Bharuch, Gujarat) and Sopara (now Nala Sopara, Mumbai) were major trading ports in the west.

For overseas trade, Taxila (now the Rawalpindi District in the north of the Punjab, Pakistan) was connected first to Kabul and then Bactria, from where it reached the Caspian Sea and the Caucasus. Another route spread from Taxila to Kandahar and Herat in Afghanistan, and on to Persia. The Satavahanas continued to expand trade to western and central Asia, Rome, Greece, China and Iran through silk routes. They traded spices, pearls, sandalwood, musk and ivory, along routes that reached all the way to South-East Asia and Ceylon (Sri Lanka).

Meanwhile, the Chola dynasty in the south had established multiple ports, including Thoothukudi, which remains an important fishery hub today. Arikamedu in Pondicherry, known as a bead-making centre, was named in a first-century Greco-Roman text. Poompuhar, mentioned in Sangam literature, traded goods with Asian and Arab countries, while Muziris, a Chera dynasty port, was crucial for trade with the Mediterranean, including North Africa, Persia, and the Greek and Roman empires.

During the Gupta period, often referred to as the Golden Era of India by historians, much of the foundation laid by previous dynasties multiplied. Ports in the south and land routes in the north bustled with activity. Coins and common currency were introduced, providing a further boost to trade, and sugarcane

and sali paddy (rice) from Bengal became particularly popular during this time. Some Indian products were so highly valued in Europe that when the Visigoths besieged Rome, they demanded a ransom from the city that included, among other things, 3000 pounds of black pepper imported from southern India.

One of the most expensive and exotic spices in the world, saffron, was a major crop in Kashmir. One popular belief says that Persians introduced saffron to India during the silk route era and encouraged its production in Kashmir, while another says an Indian Buddhist monk sowed Kashmir's first crop of saffron. Saffron was touted to have many medicinal properties; in Persia it was mixed with steaming tea to ward off melancholy and in China it was in high demand as a remedy to improve one's memory.

The Gupta government laid down laws and regulations to encourage the smooth flow of trade, and the prevailing peace across the country gave rise to advances in sciences, arts, architecture, literature and education. Under the Gupta Empire, India became a hub for trade, attracting many traders to the subcontinent who then settled there.

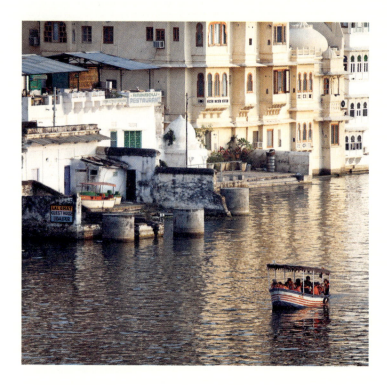

One of the early trading communities to make a home on the subcontinent was a group of merchants from different Arab countries who frequented the Malabar and Konkan coasts; many of them settled along the Malabar Coast in present-day Kerala. Their contribution to the food of Kerala is clear in Mappila cuisine, prevalent in Muslim communities in the Malabar region. Mappila cuisine includes foods such as aleesa, a sweet wheat and meat porridge; Pathiri (page 100), a soft, thin rice flatbread; and muttamala, which roughly translates to 'egg necklace' and is made from delicate strings of sweet egg yolk served with an egg-white pudding. Malabar cuisine is also famous for its ever-popular biryanis, such as mandi, a spiced rice dish with chicken or lamb cooked in a pressurised underground oven that creates a unique smoky flavour.

St Thomas the Apostle, having travelled the well-established trade routes to Malabar, arrived in Kerala in 52 CE with the aim of spreading Christianity to the coast. He converted the locals to Christianity, giving rise to a unique community in Kerala. With this unique culture came a distinctive Syrian Christian cuisine that enjoyed fish, seafood, duck, chicken and lamb dishes that were richly spiced.

From the sixteenth century onwards, Armenian traders began forming a community in the active trading port of Surat, as well as Agra, Mumbai, Chennai and Kolkata. Although only a handful of Armenians remain in present-day India, the culinary legacy they left behind continues to flourish, especially in Bengal, where an Armenian dish called Potol dolma (page 84), stuffed pointed gourd, continues to be a favourite.

The expansion of Islam sent Persian Zoroastrians to India, giving rise to the Parsi community, whose food was soon incorporated into Indian cuisine. Legend has it that an Indian king sent a full glass of milk to a Parsi community seeking asylum in an effort to convey that his kingdom was already full with its own citizens. The Persians put sugar in the milk and sent it back, likening the assimilation of their people into society as being as inconspicuous yet fruitful as the addition of sugar to milk! Today, the Parsi community are famous for their cafes, which began popping up in Mumbai in the late nineteenth century and are now part of the city's heritage. Most Parsi cafes retain their authentic menus, with dishes such as dhansak, a Parsi version of dal; bun maska and chai, the classic combination of steaming chai and a sweet, soft bun; and Patrani machi (page 88), a popular fish delicacy.

While the Chinese had traded with India and visited the subcontinent for millennia to explore Buddhist teachings, the first Chinese migrants to India did not arrive until the late eighteenth century. Many chose to settle in Kolkata, and by the early twentieth century it had a thriving Chinatown. The Chinese diaspora soon assimilated Indian beliefs and values. Today, modern Indo-Chinese food reflects local tastes, with chicken replaced by paneer and novel dishes like Chinese bhels, a hybrid of chop suey and bhelpuri, appearing on menus – most of them far from authentic.

With exports came the import of an important and now common spice in India: dar chini, or cassia bark. In Persian, 'dar' means 'spice' and 'chini' means 'from China'. Cassia bark is the one ingredient we cannot imagine Indian cuisine today without.

Trade and migration brought new produce, people and cultures, all of which changed the way those living on the Indian subcontinent ate and cooked. Produce within India became more accessible, and the cuisine became deeper, increasingly diverse and more versatile. New communities made new versions of local dishes using local produce, and local people re-created newly introduced dishes their way, making the tapestry of India's cuisine ever richer.

Kashmiri kahwa

Warm saffron and spice tea

Saffron, which has origins in the Indus Valley Civilisation and Kashmir, is known as 'the king of spices' and was highly priced even at the time of the Silk Road route during the trade and migration period in India. In Kashmir, saffron grows in abundance, and the fields of purple flowers coating the landscape against the backdrop of the mountains is one of the most beautiful sights I've ever seen. Sipping kahwa in a shikara (wooden boat) on Dal Lake might have been touristy, but it felt complete! Kahwa is made with Kashmiri green tea, saffron, whole spices, rose petals, almonds and honey. This sweet, fragrant drink is poured out of a samovar, a traditional copper tea pot that has an inbuilt section for hot coal to keep the tea warm. I first tried it in Kashmir on a roadside in the early morning in Srinagar on our way to the saffron fields, and the taste of it still lingers in my memory.

12–15 saffron threads, crushed with a mortar and pestle

1–2 g (1/32–1/16 oz) loose-leaf green tea, or 1 tea bag

2 green cardamom pods, bruised

2.5 cm (1 in) cassia bark stick

2 whole cloves

¼ teaspoon dried rose petals, plus extra to garnish

10 g (¼ oz) honey

4 almonds, thinly slivered, to serve

Utensils

Samovar (copper Kashmiri tea pot) or a pot (see method)

Charcoal, for heating (see Note)

Note

Wood chips can be used if charcoal is not available. (Light wood chips after placing them in the samovar cavity.)

If you're using a samovar, place hot coals in the centre of the samovar, then pour in 400 ml (13½ fl oz) water and add all the ingredients, except for the honey and almonds. The tea will come to the boil. Allow it to bubble gently for 5–7 minutes to develop the flavours. Pour into a cup, add the honey and almonds, and drink hot.

If you're using a pot, combine all the ingredients, except the honey and almonds, in a pot with 400 ml (13½ fl oz) water and bring it to the boil over a high heat. Reduce the heat to low and let it simmer gently for 7 minutes.

Once the flavours have developed, take it off the stove and let it sit for 1 hour, then place back over a high heat and bring to the boil again. Add the honey, then strain into cups, garnish with extra rose petals and serve with the slivered almonds.

Bhinda par ida

Eggs on okra

The Parsi community has a unique fascination with eggs. There is akuri, the famous spicy Parsi scrambled eggs, soufflés with coriander (cilantro) chutney, soft- and hard-boiled eggs on pulaos, custard baked on special occasions, or eggs on anything, called 'Kasa (anything) par (on) ida (eggs)'. This preparation is perfect for a light lunch, side or supper, and one version that stood out for me was Bhinda par ida, which follows the format of 'eggs on anything'. I have a love–hate relationship with okra; I love it deep-fried, but I don't enjoy it simply sautéed as it has a slimy texture. This dish can be made with deep-fried or sautéed okra, but I'll be sharing the deep-fried version – of course!

To prepare the bhinda, wash them in cold water then wipe each one dry with a paper towel.

Cut into 1 cm (½ in) thick slices.

Heat enough vegetable oil for deep-frying in a saucepan until it reaches 180°C (360°F) on a cooking thermometer. Fry the bhinda in batches until crisp, about 3 minutes, then set aside.

Now, add the ghee to a heavy-based skillet and place over a medium heat. Once hot, add the onion and fry until beginning to brown, then add the ginger, garlic and chilli and stir well. Add the fried okra and coriander, season with a little salt and mix well.

Reduce the heat to low and break the eggs on top of the okra. Sprinkle some salt on top of each egg, then cover the skillet with a lid. Increase the heat to medium and cook until the egg whites are set but the yolks are still runny, about 7 minutes for chicken eggs and 4 minutes for quail eggs.

Serve with bread or rice.

500 g (1 lb 2 oz) bhinda (okra; see Note)

vegetable oil, for deep-frying

15 g (½ oz) Ghee (page 38)

160 g (5½ oz) diced red onion

10 g (¼ oz) minced ginger

15 g (½ oz) minced garlic

finely diced green chilli, to taste

4–5 coriander (cilantro) stalks, finely chopped

5 chicken eggs or 10 quail eggs

Note

Always try to find okra that are thin and small; overgrown okra are very fibrous and their flavour is not as beautiful as smaller, younger okra.

Potol dolma

Fish-stuffed pointed gourd

Potol dolma, otherwise known as stuffed pointed gourd, is cooked in Bengali kitchens and is believed to have originated in the Armenian community that moved to the area and who have traded in India since the seventh century. While dolma can have various fillings, from minced (ground) meat and rice, to paneer and figs, here I have presented a version with fish as it is a quintessential and celebrated staple in the Bengali diet. The marriage between Armenian and Bengali culture is beautifully illustrated in this recipe. It is a rich and spicy dish with potol at its centre. The fish imparts its delicate flavour to the stuffing and spices, making it really moreish.

Start by making the garam masala. Toast all the spices in a dry frying pan over a low heat for 7–8 minutes. Take off the heat and leave to cool, then grind to a fine powder in a spice grinder.

To prepare the potol, use a melon scooper to gently scoop out the flesh without breaking the shell, and discard.

Heat enough oil for deep-frying in a large saucepan until it reaches 180°C (360°F) on a cooking thermometer. Once hot, flash-fry the potol in batches, for just 1 minute, making sure they don't soften too much, as they need to hold their shape for stuffing. Set aside to cool.

Add more oil to the saucepan for deep-frying if needed, then add the onions and deep-fry until golden brown. Drain on a cooling rack lined with paper towels. Blend the fried onion with a little water to make a smooth paste, then set aside.

To make the stuffing, heat 80 ml (2½ fl oz/⅓ cup) mustard oil in a frying pan over a medium heat and fry the fish for 4 minutes, then flip and cook for another 4 minutes on the other side, or until the fish is cooked through. Once cooked, remove the fish to a plate and mash with a fork.

Now, in a kadhai or heavy-based wok, heat the extra tablespoon of mustard oil over a medium heat. Once hot, add the garlic and ginger for the stuffing and cook for a few minutes until lightly brown, then add the cumin, coriander and turmeric with 1 tablespoon water and stir well. Continue cooking until the oils separate, then add the mashed fish and mix well. Take it off the heat and mix in 2 tablespoons of the fried onion paste, then leave to cool.

Fill the potol with 2 tablespoons stuffing each, or until fully stuffed, then replace the potol lids.

To make the gravy, drain the cashew nuts and blend to a smooth paste, then whisk this into the yoghurt and set aside.

500 g (1 lb 2 oz) potol (pointed gourd; see Notes), peeled, tops removed and reserved

vegetable oil, for deep-frying

500 g (1 lb 2 oz) onions, thickly sliced

Garam masala

100 g (3½ oz) whole cloves

100 g (3½ oz) cinnamon stick

300 g (10½ oz) green cardamom pods

Stuffing

80 ml (2½ fl oz/⅓ cup) mustard oil, plus 1 tablespoon extra

200 g (7 oz) boneless oily fish of your choice

1 large garlic clove, minced

1 cm (½ in) piece fresh ginger, peeled and minced

½ teaspoon ground cumin

½ teaspoon ground coriander

1 teaspoon ground turmeric

Gravy

6–7 cashew nuts, soaked in warm water

2 tablespoons plain yoghurt

2 tablespoons mustard oil

2 bay leaves

3 green cardamom pods

2.5 cm (1 in) cassia bark stick

3 whole cloves

1 teaspoon cumin seeds

2 garlic cloves, minced

1½ tablespoons minced fresh ginger

1 teaspoon ground cumin

1½ teaspoons ground coriander

1 teaspoon ground turmeric

½ teaspoon sugar

1 teaspoon Garam masala (see above)

Utensils

Spice grinder

Kadhai or heavy-based wok

Heat the mustard oil in a kadhai or heavy-based wok over a medium heat until it turns light yellow. Temper it with the bay leaves, cardamom, cassia bark, cloves and cumin seeds, followed by the garlic and ginger, and cook for 5–6 minutes or until the oil begins to separate. Add a little water if needed to stop the garlic and ginger catching.

Now add the cumin, coriander and turmeric and mix well. Cook until the oil separates.

Add the yoghurt and cashew mixture and stir quickly, seasoning the mix with some salt and the sugar. Add the remaining fried onion paste and a little water to bring the sauce to a thick pouring consistency, and bring to the boil over a medium heat. Once boiling, carefully add the stuffed dolmas.

Add 1 teaspoon garam masala and cook for another 5–6 minutes. Adjust the consistency with a little water if it begins to thicken too much, then taste and adjust the seasoning if necessary.

Serve with rice.

Notes

This recipe can be made with yellow baby (pattypan) squash if potol is not available.

The recipe for garam masala makes extra, as most spice grinders don't work effectively with small quantities. Store the left-over masala in an airtight container for up to 12 months.

Patrani machi

Fish marinated with coriander and coconut and steamed in banana leaf

The Parsi community have blended seamlessly with India's native population in places such as Mumbai and Gujarat, and have adapted their own cuisine using local produce. One of the most popular dishes in the community is Patrani machi, a flavourful fish delicacy. Patrani refers to the leaves the fish is wrapped and cooked in – in this case banana leaves – and machi, meaning fish, is coated with a coriander (cilantro) and coconut marinade, then steamed. This recipe bears a striking resemblance to macher paturi, a Bengali fish dish which is also cooked in banana leaves and uses a mustard marinade instead of coriander. The banana leaf imparts a beautiful flavour to the fish, while retaining all the moisture. This is one of my favourite methods of cooking, where very little processing is needed for the preparation of beautiful, fresh ingredients.

500 g (1 lb 2 oz) skinless, boneless white fish fillets of your choice (see Note)
1 large banana leaf

Marinade
75 g (2¾ oz) freshly grated coconut
2–3 small green chillies, destemmed
1½ bunches coriander (cilantro)
1 tablespoon cumin seeds
2 tablespoons lime or lemon juice
1 teaspoon sugar

Note
Avoid oily fish here – we're seeking a boneless white fish. I like to use Murray cod, which is a native Australian freshwater fish, but basa and pomfret also work well for this recipe.

To make the marinade, combine all the ingredients in a blender and blitz to a smooth paste.

Portion the fish fillets into 60 g (2 oz) pieces and coat them well with the marinade. Place on a plate, cover with plastic wrap and rest in the fridge for 1 hour.

Cut the banana leaf into squares large enough to wrap the fish pieces in little parcels.

Flash the banana leaves over an open flame for a few seconds to make them pliable. Now place a piece of marinated fish in the middle of each banana leaf and fold all the sides in neatly before securing with a piece of kitchen string.

Prepare a double boiler by placing a colander over a large saucepan of simmering water. Place the banana-leaf parcels in the colander, cover and cook for 12 minutes over a medium heat for thicker pieces of fish, and 7 minutes for smaller pieces. Gently squeeze the fish fillet – if it breaks easily, it's cooked.

Patrani machi can be served as an entrée or with rice as a main.

Kozhi porichathu

Chicken with onion and turmeric

Serves 4

This is a simple and delicious recipe from the Mappila community of the Malabar Coast. Mappila cuisine incorporates native ingredients like coconut, curry leaves and turmeric to create moreish dishes like this one. There are several recipes for this dish, many with the addition of garlic, ginger, green and red chilli, and more whole spices than what I have here. (Adding more spices came later to Indian cooking.) This recipe is the basic version – a simple and quick but wholesome meal.

600 g (1 lb 5 oz) red onion, sliced

10 g (¼ oz) ground black pepper

1 tablespoon ground turmeric

1 kg (2 lb 3 oz) skinless chicken pieces on the bone

3 tablespoons coconut oil

1 tablespoon Ghee (page 38)

1 curry leaf sprig, leaves stripped

Utensils
Kadhai or heavy-based wok
Vaghariyu or small pot

Bring 2 litres (68 fl oz/8 cups) water to the boil in a kadhai or heavy-based wok over a medium heat. Add the onion, increase the heat to high, and cook for 3 minutes.

Reduce the heat to medium and cook for another 5 minutes. Add the black pepper and turmeric and stir well, then add the chicken and a pinch of salt.

Cover with the lid, increase the heat to high and cook for 10 minutes, then remove the lid and stir in the coconut oil.

Bring the heat down to low and continue to cook until the liquid reduces to a thick gravy, about 25 minutes.

Heat the ghee in a vaghariyu or small pot over a medium heat until hot, then add the curry leaves and cook until they pop. Pour the oil and leaves into the chicken dish and stir well. Cook over a low heat for another 3 minutes to bring it all together.

Serve with rice.

Tharavu roast

Roast duck with gravy

The Syrian Christian community's cuisine in India is heavily influenced by local produce and techniques. The community is composed of local Brahmins who were converted to Christianity, and a few hundred Syrian Christians who had travelled there, with both communities merging through intermarriage. Christmas and Easter are prominent festivals celebrated by the community, with a spread of dishes that use spices, produce and techniques popular in Malabar cooking. One of the most popular festive dishes is a roast duck made with flavourful spices.

Portion the duck into wings, thighs and breasts. Rub with the turmeric and set aside.

For the masala, toast the cardamom pods, cassia bark and whole cloves in a dry frying pan over a low heat until fragrant, then grind the whole spices to a fine powder with the ginger, garlic, curry leaves, black pepper, vinegar and a pinch of salt.

Place the duck pieces in a deep pot and fill it with lukewarm water until the duck is almost completely submerged. Add the masala paste and mix well.

Place the pot over a medium heat and cook for 15 minutes, or until the duck is soft and the liquid has reduced by half. Stir periodically.

Remove the duck pieces and pat dry with paper towel, then set aside and allow them to come to room temperature.

Place the pot containing the liquid back over a low heat and cook for 10–15 minutes, or until the gravy coats the back of a spoon.

Heat the oil in a frying pan over a medium heat and fry the shallot until golden brown. Add the fried shallot to the gravy, keeping the oil in the pan.

Place the frying pan with the oil back over a medium heat and fry the duck pieces to caramelise the skin evenly all over.

Once fried, return the duck pieces to the gravy. Taste and adjust the seasoning, then cook for another 5 minutes over a medium heat.

Serve with rice.

2 kg (4 lb 6 oz) duck
2 tablespoons ground turmeric
5–6 green cardamom pods
1 cassia bark stick
4 whole cloves
20 g (¾ oz) piece fresh ginger, grated
30 g (1 oz) garlic cloves, peeled
2 curry leaf sprigs, leaves stripped
15 g (½ oz) ground black pepper
3 tablespoons malt vinegar
185 ml (6 fl oz/¾ cup) vegetable oil
800 g (1 lb 12 oz) shallots, thinly sliced

Kavuni arisi idli

Steamed fermented black rice batter

Serves 4

This idli is made from one of the ancient varieties of rice that grows in Tamil Nadu, which is similar to the forbidden rice, or black rice, found in China. This ancient grain is full of essential nutrients, and hence it was restricted to use only by the royals in China. In India its use is popular in fermented batter, and in recipes such as idli, dosa and uttapam. The origin of this grain is unclear, with some sources citing its arrival from China around the time of the Silk Road. This recipe makes a very delicious breakfast.

Separately wash and soak the rices and urad dal overnight in water with a pinch of fenugreek seeds in each.

The next day, drain the rice and dal, reserving the water. Blend each individually in a stone grinder or using a blender, adding enough of the soaking water to make a paste. Make sure the rices aren't totally smooth. (It's better to start with just a little water, then add more if needed.)

Mix all the batters together and add the salt. Add enough water to bring it to a thick, cake-batter consistency.

Place the batter in an airtight container, seal and leave in a warm spot to ferment for 12 hours (see Notes) or until it forms tiny air bubbles and becomes light and airy. Once fermented, the batter is ready to steam.

Pour water into an idli steamer and bring it to the boil. Grease the idli trays and fill them halfway with the batter. Drop the trays in boiling water, cover the steamer, and then cook over a medium heat for 13–15 minutes depending on how deep your idli steamer is. The water should be simmering, not boiling.

To check if the idli are cooked, pierce an idli with a skewer. If it comes out clean and the idli has puffed up, it's ready.

Take out the idli tray and let it cool for a few minutes, then remove the idli with the help of a spoon.

Serve with melted ghee, Temple sambar (page 53) or chutney.

400 g (14 oz) forbidden rice, or black rice (see Notes)
360 g (12½ oz) idli rice (see Notes)
250 g (9 oz) urad dal
10 fenugreek seeds
1 teaspoon fine sea salt
2 tablespoons vegetable oil, for greasing
3 tablespoons melted Ghee (page 38), to serve

Utensils
Stone grinder or blender
Idli steamer (see Notes)

Notes
Forbidden rice can be found in Asian grocery stores and idli rice in Indian grocery stores. Short-grain rice can be used if forbidden rice is not available.

Idli steamers can be found in Indian stores and are essential for making idlis.

If you're preparing the ferment in a warm climate, you might only need to let it sit for 6 hours.

Chilli pork

Pork with chillies and soy sauce

Some of the later generations of the Chinese communities who migrated to India in the seventeenth century opened Chinese restaurants in Kolkata, where they made food with the produce that was available to them. I had this chilli pork in Kolkata on my visit there, where we ate at one of these old Chinese establishments called Tung Nam. Among the noodles, rice, fried chicken in thick sauce, wontons and soup, this pork dish with spring onion (scallion), onion and black pepper stood out to me. The spicy, fatty pork captured the breath of the wok, with crunchy onion. As Indians today continue to modify Chinese food into a near-unrecognisable state, I love that some of these old institutions cling to authentic recipes. This is my attempt to re-create that dish.

500 g (1 lb 2 oz) boneless pork belly, fat and rind removed, cut into 2 cm (¾ in) cubes

3 garlic cloves, minced

2.5 cm (1 in) piece fresh ginger, peeled, half minced, half crushed

10 g (¼ oz) cornflour (cornstarch)

vegetable oil, for deep-frying

80 g (2¾ oz) red onion, roughly chopped

50 g (1¾ oz) spring onions (scallions), cut into 5 cm (2 in) lengths

2.5 cm (1 in) cinnamon stick

½ star anise

3 green chillies, destemmed, finely diced

½ teaspoon ground white pepper

1 tablespoon soy sauce

Utensils

Kadhai or heavy-based wok

Place the pork in a large bowl with the minced garlic and the ginger and a pinch of salt (not too much). Scatter the cornflour over the top and mix well.

Heat enough oil for deep-frying in a large saucepan until it reaches 180°C (360°F) on a cooking thermometer. Fry the pork for 2–3 minutes, or until slightly golden. Remove to a plate lined with paper towels.

Place a kadhai or heavy-based wok over a high heat, and add 2 tablespoons of the oil used for deep-frying. Add the onion, followed by the spring onion, cinnamon stick and star anise, and stir continuously. Add the fried pork and mix well.

Now add the green chilli and continue frying, stirring continuously.

Season with the white pepper and soy sauce, then cook for another 5–6 minutes over a high heat before removing from the heat to serve.

Pathiri

Rice flour flatbread

Rice has always been a central staple in southern India, and as the area is rich in varieties of the grain, even some of the breads in this region are re-created with rice! One such recipe is pathiri, a creation of the Mappila community who missed bread from their hometowns in the Middle East, and so created a bread made from rice flour. This soft bread is the perfect carrier for many thick, gravy-based preparations and stews. Enjoyed by everyone, it is soft and light, with a delicious hint of coconut milk and oil.

200 g (7 oz) rice flour, plus extra for dusting
½ teaspoon fine sea salt
2 teaspoons coconut oil
100 ml (3½ fl oz) boiling water
4 tablespoons coconut milk

Utensils
Kadhai or heavy-based wok
Dosa tava or crêpe pan
Tavetha or wooden spatula

In a dry kadhai or heavy-based wok, toast the rice flour for 7 minutes over a low heat, being sure not to let it discolour.

In a bowl, mix the toasted rice flour, salt, coconut oil and the boiling water and stir well with a spoon. Wet your hands and knead the hot dough for 5 minutes, or until it becomes soft and less sticky. Kneading is the most important part, so do it in a single stretch.

Divide the dough into 25 g (1 oz) balls and set aside under a damp tea towel (dish towel).

Dust your kitchen bench with a little rice flour and roll out each ball of dough into a thin roti about 15 cm (6 in) in diameter.

Heat your dosa tava or crêpe pan over a high heat. Once it is very hot, reduce the heat to medium and add a pathiri. Cook until bubbles appear on the surface of the dough, then flip it over using a tavetha or wooden spatula and cook the other side, pressing the centre of the pathiri gently with a bundled-up tea towel. As it rises, press gently all over the pathiri to help it puff up evenly.

Brush the pathiri with some coconut milk and store immediately in a tea towel to keep it soft. Repeat with the remaining dough.

Serve your pathiri with pickles or other preparations with gravy.

Modaka

Pastry stuffed with coconut and jaggery

During the Gupta era, in the fourth century to the sixth, India had well-developed trade routes, with traders and foreign communities living together. The ancient scripts and texts of the Gupta era list a number of vegetarian food items which became popular under the influence of rising Buddhism and Jainism. During this period, a vegetarian diet soon became the norm for as much as half of the population. In the Gupta Empire, people mostly ate vegetables, cereals, fruits and breads, and drank milk. Sugar cubes were also produced at the time, so more people began to eat sugar and prepare sugary desserts. The most popular sweet dishes of the Gupta era are modakas, which can still be found in Orissa. Called manda pitha, they are made during festivities or Puja, a worshipping ritual. Modakas are said to be one of the favourite dishes of Lord Ganesha, as well as Buddha, and are made of fried or steamed wheat or rice flour shells with a jaggery and coconut filling.

500 g (1 lb 2 oz/2 cups) Ghee (page 38), for deep-frying

Dough
125 g (4½ oz) wholemeal (whole-wheat) flour
25 g (1 oz) plain (all-purpose) flour
pinch of fine sea salt
2 tablespoons melted Ghee (page 38)
oil, for shaping the dough

Filling
150 g (5½ oz) freshly grated coconut
150 g (5½ oz) jaggery
¼ teaspoon ground cardamom

Utensils
Kadhai or heavy-based wok

To prepare the dough, combine the flours and salt in a bowl. Mix in the melted ghee.

Add 150 ml (5 fl oz) water and knead the dough for 5 minutes, or until it becomes firm. Cover the dough and rest for 1 hour.

To make the filling, add the coconut and jaggery to a kadhai or heavy-based wok set over a low heat and stir continuously until the jaggery melts and caramelises the coconut, about 10 minutes.

Keep stirring for another 3 minutes until the liquid reduces but hasn't completely evaporated. Turn off the heat and allow the mixture to cool. Add the ground cardamom and mix well.

Divide the dough into 15 g (½ oz) portions. Oil your hands and flatten each piece into a 7 cm (2¾ in) disc with the palm of your hand and fingers. Place ½ tablespoon of the coconut mix in the centre. Bring the sides together and pinch to seal. Repeat with the remaining dough and filling.

Heat the ghee for deep-frying in a kadhai or heavy-based wok over a medium heat until it reaches 150°C (300°F) on a cooking thermometer. Add a few stuffed modakas at a time to the hot ghee and deep-fry for 10 minutes, turning continuously to make sure they are evenly cooked and a deep golden-brown colour. Remove and drain on paper towel.

Modakas can be eaten warm or at room temperature, and are delicious served with tea.

MUGHAL
INVASION

The next chapter in the evolution of Indian cuisine is perhaps the most influential one, while also being the bloodiest and most turbulent for the local Indian population. In the Middle Ages most countries were either being invaded or invading others, and India was no exception. With its abundance of natural resources and desirable geographical location, India was a very attractive area to capture. The north of India was constantly being attacked by dynasties, such as Greek, Kushan, Ghaznavid, Ghurid, Khilji, Lodhi and more, many of which were successful in establishing dynasties in the North.

By the time Babur, a descendant of Timur and Genghis Khan born in Uzbekistan, defeated Ibrahim Lodi, the Sultan of Delhi, at the First Battle of Panipat in 1526 and founded the Mughal Empire, India had lost its tolerance towards invaders, and battles fought during this time were deadlier than ever. According to Babur's autobiography, *Baburnama*, his campaign in north-west India targeted Hindus and Sikhs as well as apostates (non-Sunni sects of Islam), and an immense number were killed. It was perhaps in this era that the native population began to be referred to as Hindus, as before this period, the term 'Hindu' did not exist. The Mughals branded India as Hindustan, and people living there as Hindus, which in reality comprised several distinct religions, castes and cultures.

The Hindus, with their ancient and strong religion, were not ready to give up their culture, and the Mughals, with their equally strong and influential religion of Islam, were not ready to Indianise themselves. Temples that were sacred to the native people were destroyed in this era, and many mosques were built. Massacres were abundant and brutal, and many communities were forced to convert their religion to be spared death and looting. This period laid the foundation for the divide between the Hindus and Muslims in the subcontinent. The Mughals ruled India for about 300 years, and after capturing the North they started spreading to the East, West and South. However, the Rajputs, Peshwas, Cholas, Marathas, Pandyas, Pallavas, Palas, Gurjaras and other native dynasties never let the Mughals take hold of the entirety of India.

Soon the Mughals realised that the Hindus could only be captured bit by bit, and perhaps it was impossible to separate religion from them, so Babur's descendants – Humayun, Akbar, Jahangir, Shah Jahan and Bahadur Shah Zafar – all made attempts to win the hearts of locals to secure their dynasty. Akbar married Rajput princess Jodha and gave Rajputs seats in his parliament. The Mughals called India their home, unlike the British, who were just interested in looting the nation.

The Mughals were originally from Central Asia and spoke Persian, as it was the high-culture language of the time, and they drew culinary influences from their neighbours, the Tajiks, Kyrgyz and Tatras, Turkmens, Ukrainians, Russians, Armenians and Azerbaijans. The Mughal era was well documented by many literary publications, such as *Baburnama*, *Ain-i-Akbari*, *Tuzk-e-Jahangiri* and other records, and literature described the food habits, ingredients and dishes, as well as the scale of grandeur and lavish lives the Mughals lived in the era.

In *Ain-i-Akbari*, Abul Fazl writes that the diet of Mughals heavily relied on rice, wheat, gram, barley, lentils and ghee. Spices were sparsely used, with the most common ones being cumin, coriander, ginger, pepper, cinnamon, cloves and fennel. Dried fruits and nuts were used in large quantities, typically almonds, pistachio nuts, walnuts, dried apricots, plums and raisins. While some of the dried fruits were imported from Central Asia and Persia, many fruits were introduced and then cultivated in India. Sweet grapes, melons and pineapples were brought in by Babur and Akbar, who later set up royal orchards to satisfy their love of Central Asian fruits. Desserts like khubani ka meetha (preserved apricots with cream) were popular at the time, along with halwas that were made with dried fruits and reduced milk. Exotic fresh and dried fruits still remain a prime gift in present-day India for weddings and festivals.

Food was cooked in ghee, almond oil, apricot oil and grapeseed oil. Sheep, goats and fowl were fed aromatic herbs, silver, gold, rose petals and saffron to make the meat fragrant. Food was perfumed with rose water, camphor, orange leaves, sandalwood and fennel leaves. In current times, Awadhi cuisine in India best represents the food from this era. Food for royals was often cooked in gold, silver and earthenware pots. The slow-cooking style, which can now be found in the biryanis and pulaos cooked in Hyderabad, Delhi, Chettinad and many other parts of India, was introduced by the royal cooks.

In Jahangir's period, between 1605 and 1627, the cooks from Samarkand brought their overnight slow-cooking method on a wood fire to Kashmir. The fascination with slow-cooked meats is present year-round in India, but especially during Eid, when dishes like nihari and haleem, both slow-cooked meat stews, are prepared by shops near the mosques.

Breads cooked during the Mughal era were leavened and dairy was added in abundance in the form of ghee, yoghurt and milk. Breads like Sheermal (page 134), which is made with milk and dipped in ghee; Mughaliya paratha, which is bread stuffed with minced (ground) meat; and rumali roti, a bread as thin as a napkin, are all still hugely popular.

Kebabs were also introduced by the Mughals, and they developed several varieties of kebabs in India, like shami, mahi, galawati, shikampuri (see page 124) and more. Malpuas (page 58) were a treat, though jalebis soon took over as a crowd favourite when Mughaliya kitchens introduced the delicacy to India.

The culinary contribution in this era included techniques as well as entire dishes that stayed and were then incorporated into Indian cuisine. Mughaliya cuisine (the cuisine of the Mughals) is distinct in its flavour profile, placing emphasis on textures and fragrances, such as those of rose petals, musk, saffron, vetiver roots, stone flowers and galangal. These are unique spices which are still not brought out on a regular basis. Turmeric is scarcely used in this cuisine, as it was a native Indian ingredient and not easily adopted. Even now, a good biryani is believed not to have turmeric or red chilli in it.

Additionally, the chaats (street foods that are sweet, sour, spicy and textured; see page 115) that are believed to have originated during this era now use chillies in abundance.

The heavy use of onion and garlic is something that Mughaliya cuisine incorporated extensively, be that fried onion or the ginger and garlic paste at the start of recipes and marinades. This is not seen as a must in other regional Indian cuisines, except the Punjabi food served in restaurants, which is a mix of the best of all worlds and combines the richness of Mughaliya with the spice blends of Bhartiya cuisine.

Nut pastes used to thicken sauces were another addition from this era and are now widely used. Silver and gold were incorporated into desserts and savoury dishes as a symbol of royalty, and gold coins and pearls were added to drinking water. Many of these traditions are still carried out today.

Meat and poultry stood at the centre of each dish – there is even a record of a dessert with goat meat in it. The Bhartiya population, with their vegetarian diet, were now surrounded by meat-eating communities, and sophisticated butchery and preparation of meat dishes came with them. While the ancient Indians did cook and eat meat, the variety of meats and attention to detail was brought by the Mughals. Dishes like musallam (see page 131), which was an ultimate test of butchery, were created at this time, where smaller animals and birds were stuffed inside bigger animals and presented whole to royalty. Techniques of softening the meat with spices and fruits, like raw papaya, smoking the meat with coal, cooking meats in tandoors, or even emulsifying meat with fat and pulses by slow cooking in dishes like haleem and harissa (see page 128), were contributions that changed the food of Hindustan forever.

113

Papdi chaat

Crackers topped with chutney, potatoes and sev

It is believed chaat was invented during the Mughal era when the Hakim (royal doctor) of Shah Jahan ordered the population of Delhi to eat deep-fried, pungent and spicy food along with yoghurt. Whatever the reason for his order, chaat is guaranteed to uplift your mood, offering a whirlwind of flavours and textures in one bite: sweet, sour, fresh, spicy, crunchy and soft.

Combine all the papdi ingredients in a bowl with 100 ml (3½ fl oz) water and bring together with your hands into a stiff dough. Knead for 5–6 minutes, then set aside to rest for 1 hour.

Roll the dough out into a large, thin sheet about 3 mm (⅛ in) thick and prick it all over with a fork. Cut out circles of dough with a 5 cm (2 in) round cookie cutter.

Heat enough oil for deep-frying in a saucepan over a medium heat until the oil reaches 140°C (285°F). Deep-fry the papdi in batches until crisp then remove and drain on a paper towel. You can also bake these in the oven at 160°C (320°F) for 10 minutes, or until crisp.

To make the green chutney, add all the ingredients to a blender and blitz until smooth. Add a little water if necessary to adjust the consistency; it should be the pouring consistency of tomato sauce (ketchup).

For the tamarind chutney, add all the ingredients to a saucepan with 1 litre (34 fl oz/4 cups) water. Season with salt, then bring to the boil over a medium heat. Mix and mash with a wooden spoon. Reduce the heat to low. Cook for 10 minutes, then remove from the heat and let it come to room temperature.

Transfer the mixture to a blender and blitz until smooth, then pass it through a fine-mesh sieve. It should have the consistency of thick tomato sauce (ketchup). Add a little water to loosen during and after blending, and adjust the seasoning if necessary.

Place your papdi on a flat serving tray and sprinkle the diced boiled potatoes on top. Scatter the onion and kala chana over too. Drizzle with the green chutney, tamarind chutney and yoghurt. Now, sprinkle the nylon sev all over the papdi, followed by the coriander, cumin, chilli and chaat masala. Serve immediately.

Notes

Papdi and tamarind chutney can also be store-bought, but I recommend making your green chutney at home to ensure it's super fresh. You can use store-bought chaat masala or, to make your own, mix 2 tablespoons cumin seeds (toasted and ground), 1 tablespoon coriander seeds (toasted and ground), 1 tablespoon Indian black salt, 2 tablespoons dried mango powder and ½ teaspoon ground white pepper.

Kala chana is a type of chickpea native to India. It is smaller and darker in colour than regular chickpeas. Nylon sev can be found at Indian grocers.

Papdi

150 g (5½ oz/1 cup) wholemeal (whole-wheat) flour

15 g (½ oz) besan (chickpea flour)

pinch of caraway seeds

2 tablespoons vegetable oil, plus extra for deep-frying

Green chutney

2 bunches coriander (cilantro), leaves picked

½ bunch mint, leaves picked

2 large garlic cloves, peeled

15 g (½ oz) toasted peanuts

2 green chillies, destemmed

½ tablespoon toasted cumin seeds

1 teaspoon Indian black salt

⅛ teaspoon citric acid

2 tablespoons vegetable oil

1 tablespoon sugar

3 tablespoons lime juice

Tamarind chutney

100 g (3½ oz) tamarind pulp

100 g (3½ oz) pitted dates

100 g (3½ oz) jaggery

5 g (⅛ oz) ground fennel seeds

10 g (¼ oz) ground coriander

10 g (¼ oz) red chilli powder

5 g (⅛ oz) ground cumin

To serve

20–25 Papdi (see above)

1 potato, peeled, boiled and diced

½ small red onion, finely diced

120 g (4½ oz/¼ cup) kala chana (Bengal gram; see Notes), soaked and boiled

2–3 tablespoons Green chutney (see above)

2 teaspoons Tamarind chutney (see above)

200 g (7 oz) whisked plain yoghurt

80 g (2¾ oz) nylon sev (see Notes)

2 coriander (cilantro) sprigs, finely chopped

pinch of ground cumin

pinch of red chilli powder

½ teaspoon chaat masala (see Notes)

Samosa warqi

Serves 2

Layered pastry stuffed with smoked spiced lamb

'Samushak' or 'sambusak' was a dish cooked in the royal kitchens of the Delhi Sultanate. Several scripts from the era describe a filled flaky pastry which is then deep-fried. Lamb, chicken and egg were popular fillings that were seasoned with spices and textured with nuts and raisins. The pastry would sometimes be a simple single layer, while at other times a flaky, multi-layered preparation. This dish was later reinvented with similar spices and a potato filling as the samosa, and it became one of the most popular Indian foods. Here, I am sharing a samosa with a celebratory filling often made during Ramadan. It has a smoky, meaty filling with raisins and nuts encased in delicious flaky pastry.

Combine 50 g (1¾ oz) ghee and the flour in a small bowl, then set aside.

Start with the pastry so it can rest while you make the filling. Add the flour, ghee and salt to a bowl, and mix well. Working a little at a time, add approximately 100 ml (3½ fl oz) water and mix with your hand to form a smooth dough. Remove from the bowl and knead on a lightly dusted bench for about 10 minutes, or until the dough is stretchy. Cover with a damp cloth and rest for at least 20 minutes.

Roll the dough out to a 20 cm (8 in) square, then spread about 1 teaspoon of the flour and ghee mix evenly on the rolled dough. Fold the dough in half to make a rectangle, then spread another teaspoon of the flour and ghee mix evenly on the dough, before folding it in half again to make a square. Pinch the sides to seal them. Cover the dough with a tea towel (dish towel) and refrigerate for 15 minutes.

Remove the dough and roll out again to a 20 cm (8 in) square and repeat the previous steps. After resting in the fridge roll out the dough a third time to a 20 cm (8 in) square. Cut into 10 cm (4 in) squares. Lay the squares flat on your dusted benchtop and cover with a tea towel.

Make the garam masala by toasting all the ingredients in a dry frying pan over a low heat for about 6 minutes, or until fragrant. Stir continuously to avoid burning the spices. Remove from the pan and set aside to come to room temperature. Once cool, grind to a smooth powder with a spice grinder or mortar and pestle.

To make the filling, heat the ghee in a frying pan over a medium heat. Add the onion and fry for 10 minutes, or until golden brown.

60 g (2 oz) Ghee (page 38), for layering paste and smoking

25 g (1 oz) plain (all-purpose) flour, for layering paste

1 egg, beaten

vegetable oil, for deep-frying

Green chutney (see page 115), to serve

Pastry

150 g (5½ oz/1 cup) plain (all-purpose) flour, plus extra for dusting

10 g (¼ oz) Ghee (page 38)

1 teaspoon fine salt

Garam masala

15 whole black peppercorns

7 whole cloves

5 green cardamom pods

5 cm (2 in) cinnamon stick

Filling

2 tablespoons Ghee (page 38)

½ red onion, thinly sliced

1½ tablespoons minced ginger

1 tablespoon minced garlic

1 teaspoon coriander seeds, toasted and coarsely crushed

1 teaspoon Garam masala (see above)

2 whole cloves

250 g (9 oz) minced (ground) lamb

1 tablespoon sliced almonds

1 tablespoon sliced pistachio nuts

1 tablespoon raisins

Utensils

Spice grinder or mortar and pestle

Charcoal, for smoking (see Note)

Note

Wood chips can be used if charcoal is not available.

Continued next page →

Add the ginger and garlic and cook for another 1–2 minutes until fragrant and lightly toasted.

Now add the coriander seeds followed by the lamb, then add 1 teaspoon garam masala and mix well. Fry for 20–25 minutes until all the liquid has evaporated, then season to taste with salt. Remove from the heat and allow the mix to come to room temperature.

Next, we want to smoke the lamb mixture. To do this, add the lamb mixture to a deep glass or steel bowl. Place a piece of aluminium foil on top of the lamb mixture in the middle. Heat a small piece of coal either on the stove top or with a blowtorch until it is red hot and place on the aluminium foil. Melt the remaining tablespoon of ghee and pour it on top of the coal. Top with the two cloves, then quickly cover the bowl with another piece of foil. Leave to smoke for 15 minutes.

Uncover the bowl and take out the coal and foil.

Add the almonds, pistachios and raisins and mix well.

Now take one square of pastry and place 25 g (1 oz) of the lamb mixture in the middle.

Brush the pastry edge with the beaten egg, then fold in half and press the pastry to enclose the filling. Repeat with the remaining dough and filling.

Heat enough oil for deep-frying in a large saucepan until the oil reaches 160°C (320°F) on a cooking thermometer. Working in batches, drop the pastries into the hot oil and fry until golden brown, turning halfway through. Remove and drain on paper towel.

Serve with green chutney.

Shirin pulao

Rice and goat with aromatic spices

Biryani, biryan, pulao and pilaf are all preparations with hundreds of combinations and all consist of meat and rice. There are numerous stories about their origin, and which is correct is unknown. Each interpretation of a pulao has its own spice profile. Some include potatoes, some don't, some use chicken, and some use goat or mutton. It is always a celebratory dish, and the presentation is always special and theatrical, too. Generally, it is made in a big handi (a cooking vessel for biryani) over a wood fire, but at home small pots will work just as well. The success of this dish is measured by the fluffiness of the rice and the softness of the meat. This version uses goat meat and fragrant spices with fresh citrus.

Preheat the oven to 120°C (250°F).

Start by making the garam masala. Mix all the spices together, tip into a roasting tin and toast in the oven for 10 minutes. Leave to cool, then grind in a spice grinder. This will yield approximately 750 g (1 lb 11 oz) garam masala, which can be stored in an airtight container for up to 3 months.

For the brown onion paste, blend both ingredients together in a bowl to form a thick paste.

Wash and drain the rice and place in a saucepan with double the quantity of salted water. Bring to the boil over a medium heat and cook for 25 minutes, or until the rice is about 70 per cent cooked. Drain, and set aside.

If you are using the handi (pan) method to cook this recipe, make a rough dough by combining the atta flour with 200 ml (7 fl oz) water in a bowl. Knead to bring together, then set aside underneath a damp tea towel.

Combi-oven method

Preheat the oven to 180°C (360°F).

Place the goat in a deep roasting tin and roast in the oven for 25–30 minutes until the fat has rendered. (If your goat doesn't have a lot of fat on it, you can skip this step.)

Tip the excess fat out of the pan, then add enough salted water to completely submerge the meat. Seal tightly with aluminium foil and bake at 140°C (285°F) for 40 minutes, then remove and set aside.

Add the ghee to a frying pan set over a medium heat. Once hot, add the ginger and garlic and fry for 1 minute.

1.5 kg (3 lb 5 oz) rice (sella basmati; available at Indian grocers), soaked in cold water for 1 hour

1 kg (2 lb 3 oz) bone-in goat shoulder

50 g (1¾ oz) Ghee (page 38)

50 g (1¾ oz) minced garlic

30 g (1 oz) minced ginger

300 g (10½ oz) Brown onion paste (see below)

15 g (½ oz) Garam masala (see below)

25 g (1 oz) diced fried onion

1 orange, peeled and segmented

1 blood orange, peeled and segmented

1 tablespoon barberries

1 tablespoon dried edible rose petals

2–3 mint sprigs, finely chopped

½ teaspoon saffron threads, soaked in 3 teaspoons milk then crushed to a paste

2 tablespoons slivered pistachio nuts

5 coriander (cilantro) sprigs, finely chopped

Garam masala

200 g (7 oz) cumin seeds

150 g (5½ oz) coriander seeds

25 g (1 oz) dried edible rose petals

30 g (1 oz) patthar ke phool (black stone flower)

20 g (¾ oz) cinnamon stick

75 g (2¾ oz) whole cloves

25 g (1 oz) black cardamom pods

50 g (1¾ oz) green cardamom pods

10 g (¼ oz) star anise

75 g (2¾ oz) fennel seeds

75 g (2¾ oz) whole black peppercorns

15 g (½ oz) dried bay leaves

20 g (¾ oz) javitri (mace)

large pinch of ground nutmeg

Brown onion paste

150 g (5½ oz) deep-fried brown onion, sliced (see Note, overleaf)

150 g (5½ oz) plain yoghurt

Continued next page →

Now add the braised goat and cook for 2–3 minutes. If the meat begins to stick, add a little of the braising stock from the tin to loosen.

Add the brown onion paste and cook for a few minutes, then add 3 tablespoons garam masala, mix well and check the seasoning. Cook for another 2–3 minutes until the liquid has slightly reduced, then take it off the heat.

Increase the oven temperature to 180°C (360°F).

Place the meat in the base of a deep roasting tin and cover with the rice. Scatter the diced fried onion over the rice, then top with the orange and blood orange segments, barberries, rose petals and mint. Sprinkle the saffron water evenly on top and cover the tin with aluminium foil.

Bake for 40 minutes, then remove from the oven and set aside to rest for 10 minutes.

Carefully remove the foil and garnish with the slivered pistachios and coriander. Scoop the rice and meat into a bowl and enjoy with raita or raw onion.

Handi, or pan, method

Heat 15 g (½ oz) of the ghee in a handi or large pan, add the goat and render the fat over a low heat.

Tip out the excess fat and return the meat to the handi. Cover the meat with salted water and braise over a medium–low heat for 1½ hours, stirring every now and then. Top up the water if necessary to keep the meat submerged.

Remove the goat from the pan and set aside. Reserve the braising stock.

Add the remaining ghee to the handi and set it back over a medium heat. Once the ghee is hot, add the ginger and garlic and fry for 1–2 minutes.

Return the braised goat to the pan and cook for another 2–3 minutes. If the meat begins to stick, add a little of the braising stock to loosen.

Add the brown onion paste and cook for a few minutes, then add 3 tablespoons garam masala, mix well and check the seasoning. Cook for 2–3 minutes until the liquid has slightly reduced. Take it off the heat.

Spread the meat evenly in the base of the handi and cover with the rice. Scatter the diced fried onion over the rice, then top with the orange and blood orange segments, barberries, rose petals and mint. Sprinkle the saffron water evenly on top.

Roll out a thick string of dough and place it on the top lip of the handi. Cover with a flat lid and press down slightly to create an airtight seal.

Reduce the heat to low and place some hot coals on top of the lid. Cook for 25 minutes. Remove from the heat and rest for 10 minutes.

Carefully open the lid by inserting the back of a spoon between the lid and dough – be careful, as the steam will be very hot.

Remove the lid, discard the dough and garnish the pulao with the slivered pistachios and coriander.

Scoop the meat and rice into a serving bowl and serve with raita or raw onion.

Dough (handi/pan method only)

500 g (1 lb 2 oz/3⅓ cups) atta flour,
or plain (all-purpose) flour

Utensils (combi-oven method)

Spice grinder

Combi oven

Utensils (handi/pan method)

Spice grinder

Handi or pan big enough to hold the meat
in one layer

Flat handi or pan lid

Charcoal, for heat

Note

To deep-fry onions and shallots, soak
sliced onion or shallot in cold water with
a little salt to stabilise the acids, then drain
well and deep-fry. This will give the onion
or shallot good, even colouring.

Shikampuri kebab

Spiced lamb patty stuffed with hung yoghurt and mint

Meat has been consumed by Indians since ancient times, but the Mughaliya way of consuming meat was special. Lamb, beef and poultry were given closer attention than other meat, and the variety of dishes made from meat was greater than that of many of the regional cuisines of India. Kebab is one such Mughal preparation. Each state where Mughals once reigned has its own special kebab: Lucknow boasts melt-in-the-mouth galouti kebabs, Delhi swears by the softness of shami kebabs, and the shikampuri kebab demands attention. 'Shikam' means 'belly' in Urdu, and 'pur' means 'filled'; these kebabs are made with minced (ground) lamb and filled with hung yoghurt. You can replace the lamb with jackfruit to make this recipe vegetarian.

Toast the cardamom, cumin seeds, peppercorns, cinnamon stick and cloves in a dry frying pan over a low heat until fragrant. Remove from the heat and allow to cool. Once the spices come to room temperature, grind them to a powder in a spice grinder.

Place the chana dal in a saucepan and cover with double the quantity of salted water. Bring to the boil over a medium heat and cook for 15 minutes, or until soft but not mushy. Drain, and leave to come to room temperature.

Heat the oil in a frying pan over a medium heat and cook the garlic for 1 minute, then add the lamb mince and fry for 25–30 minutes until cooked through. Add the ground spices and cook until the liquid has fully evaporated, then remove from the heat and cool to room temperature.

Pass the cooled mince mixture through a mincer fitted with the fine attachment.

Pass the chana dal through the mincer, as well as the blanched almonds and fried onion. Mix with the lamb and 1 egg until you have a homogenous mixture. The mince mixture should be soft enough to hold stuffing but not too wet. Add the additional egg if necessary to achieve the right texture. Divide the mixture into 8 equal balls.

For the filling, combine all the ingredients in a bowl and mix well, then divide into 8 equal portions.

Lightly oil your hands and flatten a ball of meat into a disc. Add a portion of filling to the centre and carefully fold the meat mixture up around the filling and enclose. You want to make a flat patty or kebab here with the filling inside. Repeat with the remaining meat and filling, then chill the kebabs in the fridge for 10 minutes.

Heat enough ghee for shallow-frying in a flat tava or pan over a medium heat and shallow-fry the kebabs for 3–4 minutes on either side until golden.

Serve with green chutney, raw onion, green chillies, lime wedges and Sheermal.

2 black cardamom pods

12 green cardamom pods

10 g (¼ oz) black cumin seeds

15 g (½ oz) whole black peppercorns

6 cm (2½ in) cinnamon stick

8 whole cloves

100 g (3½ oz) chana dal (split chickpeas), soaked for 1 hour

80 ml (2½ fl oz/⅓ cup) vegetable oil, plus extra for oiling

16 large garlic cloves, chopped

1 kg (2 lb 3 oz) minced (ground) lamb

40 g (1½ oz) blanched almonds

2 large onions, sliced and deep-fried until golden (see Note, page 121)

2 eggs

approx. 3 tablespoons Ghee (page 38), for shallow-frying

Green chutney (page 115), to serve

1 raw onion, sliced; green chillies; and lime wedges, to serve

Sheermal (page 134), to serve

Filling

1 small red onion, finely diced

6 mint sprigs, leaves finely chopped

8 coriander (cilantro) sprigs, leaves picked

4 green chillies, destemmed and finely chopped

400 g (14 oz) hung yoghurt (see Note)

Utensils

Spice grinder

Mincer (meat grinder)

Tava or flat pan

Note

To make hung yoghurt, spoon yoghurt into a muslin (cheesecloth) and tie the muslin closed. Place the muslin in a fine-mesh sieve, then rest the sieve over a deep bowl to collect the whey. Refrigerate overnight. The next day, scrape the hung yoghurt from the muslin. Discard the whey.

Nadru yakhni

Lotus roots in yoghurt sauce and mild spices

The Kashmiri Wazwan style of cooking is dramatically different to other styles on the subcontinent. Most Indian regions have recipes that begin with oil in a kadhai, or wok, followed by adding whole and ground spices, garlic, ginger and onion, followed by braising meat. In Wazwan cooking, spices are added to stocks and sauces that might have started in a pot and are simmering away instead of extracting the flavours of spices in oils. The meat is almost always cooked in water with spices, with any left-over liquid reserved as a yakhni (stock) to be used in other applications in place of water. Many recipes prefer to use garlic water instead of crushed garlic, ground ginger instead of fresh ginger, and saffron is used generously too.

To date, Wazwan is prepared by Wazas (chefs of the cuisine), and about 36 items are prepared, most of them eaten with rice, including vegetarian options, fish and meat such as mutton. On my visit to Kashmir, I had the fortune to sample Nadru yakhni made by Muhammad, the chef at the hotel we stayed at. It was silky, warm but not spicy, and very flavourful. I asked Muhammad for the recipe, and over his face flashed a twinge of disbelief, pride, joy and surprise. He kindly wrote it down on a piece of paper, which I still carry in my wallet.

500 g (1 lb 2 oz) lotus root
1 egg
500 g (1 lb 2 oz/2 cups) natural yoghurt
5 g (⅛ oz) cassia bark
10 g (¼ oz) green cardamom pods
1 teaspoon ground fennel seeds
1 teaspoon ground coriander seeds
2 garlic cloves, crushed
30 g (1 oz) Ghee (page 38)
2 shallots, sliced
½ teaspoon dried mint

Clean the lotus root by scraping the outer skin, then wash it thoroughly to remove any dirt. Slice the root thinly.

Bring a large saucepan of salted water to the boil and cook the lotus root for about 20 minutes, or until tender. Drain and set aside.

In a saucepan, beat the egg and yoghurt together until smooth. Add 500 ml (17 fl oz/2 cups) water and beat again until smooth. Place over a medium heat and bring to the boil, stirring continuously so the mixture doesn't split.

Once boiling, reduce the heat to low. (You can stop stirring at this point as it shouldn't split after it has boiled.)

Add the cassia bark, cardamom pods, fennel and coriander seeds, and the garlic and stir well. Simmer over a medium heat for 10 minutes.

Place a small frying pan over a medium heat and add the ghee. Shallow-fry the shallot until dark golden, then pour the ghee and onion mix into the yoghurt mixture. Top up with a little water if it begins to reduce too much.

Add the lotus root to the yoghurt mixture and cook for another 10 minutes over a low heat, then remove. Finish with the dried mint and serve with rice.

Kashmiri harissa

Serves 4

Slow-cooked mutton with spices

This nourishing winter breakfast dish is made from pounded mutton, rice and spices. Originating in Central Asia, it is believed to have been introduced to Kashmir in the fourteenth century. I was fortunate to have been able to taste this delicacy during my visit to Srinagar. On a cold morning, I stumbled across this small harissa shop with no obvious frontage or signs. It was a small room with an elevated platform that had a pot built into it. The rest of the pot was under the platform where the wood was burnt to cook the harissa. The artisan sat on the platform, pounding the meat, announcing that it takes 6 hours to cook harissa and that he had started cooking it last night. He scooped the meat out of the pot, poured hot mustard oil on it, then served it with bread. The meat melted in my mouth, along with the mellow spices. This recipe is my attempt to mimic the real deal.

300 g (10½ oz) short-grain white rice

375 ml (12½ fl oz/1½ cups) mustard oil

8 banana shallots, thinly sliced

3 large red onions, thinly sliced

4.5 kg (9 lb 15 oz) bone-in mutton thigh, or goat thigh, washed in cold water

45 g (1½ oz) fennel seeds

4 cm (1½ in) cinnamon stick

10 whole cloves

3 black cardamom pods

10 green cardamom pods

3 garlic cloves, chopped

15 g (½ oz) cumin seeds

Note

You can finish the dish with flambéed mustard oil if you like. Heat 80 ml (2½ fl oz/⅓ cup) mustard oil in a small saucepan with a few drops of water and heat, tilting the pan slightly to catch the liquid on fire. Pour it over the harissa just before serving.

Wash the rice four or five times, then soak in water for 5 hours. Drain and add the rice to a blender, then blitz to a paste (add a little water if necessary). Set aside.

Heat the mustard oil in a saucepan until it reaches 180°C (360°F) on a cooking thermometer and fry the shallots for 7–10 minutes, then remove and set aside.

Add one sliced red onion to the oil and deep-fry for 10 minutes, then set aside. Reserve 250 ml (8½ fl oz/1 cup) of the mustard oil.

Place the mutton in a deep pot set over a medium heat and add 4 litres (135 fl oz/16 cups) water. Simmer for 1 hour, skimming any foam or impurities that rise to the surface, until the water is clear.

Place the fennel seeds, cinnamon stick, cloves and cardamom in a piece of muslin (cheesecloth) and tie up with kitchen string to create a pouch. Drop this into the pot, along with the garlic and the remaining sliced onion, and mix well.

Cover and cook over a medium heat for 1–2 hours until the meat is soft and falling off the bone. Add more water if necessary to keep the meat submerged. Remove from the heat and leave to cool to room temperature.

Remove the spice pouch and strain the stock and reserve. Top up the stock with water if necessary to bring it up to about 4 litres (135 fl oz/16 cups). Remove the meat from the bones, and discard the bones.

Add the meat and one-quarter of the reserved stock to a large pot and set it back over a medium heat.

Using a wooden pestle or a spoon, mash the meat and add another one-quarter of the stock. Add the cumin seeds and keep mashing.

Next, add the rice paste and another one-quarter of the stock, mixing and mashing as you go. Stir continuously to make sure no lumps form in the process.

Add the fried onion with the remaining stock and continue mashing and stirring. Cook until you have a very soft, thick consistency. If you find you need a little more liquid, you can always add some hot water in place of the stock. Taste and adjust the seasoning if needed.

Add three-quarters of the fried shallots and the reserved mustard oil and continue mashing.

After 5–7 minutes, give it a taste and if it is melting in your mouth, it is ready. The entire process of mixing and mashing may take up to 1½ hours, so be patient. Remove the harissa from the heat.

Spread the cooked harissa on a serving plate and sprinkle with the remaining fried shallots. Serve with Sheermal (page 134).

Murg musallam

Whole stuffed chicken

'Musallam' means full, complete or entire. This recipe is for a murg (chicken) musallam, although other poultry can be used. It is a celebratory dish and one of the most famous from Awadhi cuisine, which comes from Awadh – present-day north Uttar Pradesh – where the cuisine was heavily influenced by Persian cooking. Whole birds were stuffed with minced (ground) lamb and chicken, rice and nuts. The cuisines of this region are fragrant, and the flavours delicate.

Make the brine by bringing 2 litres (68 fl oz/8 cups) water to the boil in a large saucepan. Add the fennel seeds, ginger, peppercorns and salt. Remove from the heat and leave to cool. Place the chicken in the brine and refrigerate overnight.

To make the marinade, mix all the ingredients together in a large bowl and season lightly with salt.

Drain the chicken and pat dry with paper towel. Place the chicken in the marinade, ensuring that it is well coated both inside and out. Cover the bowl with plastic wrap and refrigerate for at least 2 hours.

To make the stuffing, toast the cardamom and cassia bark lightly in a dry frying pan over a low heat until fragrant. Remove and leave to cool, then blend to a fine powder in a spice grinder.

Heat the ghee in a frying pan over a medium heat, add the onion and cook for 10 minutes, or until lightly golden. Now add the chicken mince and cook for 10 minutes until it releases its liquid. Add the ground cardamom and cassia bark and season well. Once the mince is fully cooked, add the slivered almonds, pistachio and cashew nuts, and the raisins, and mix well. Take the mince off the heat and leave it to come to room temperature. Add the chopped coriander and mix well.

Preheat the oven to 180°C (360°F).

Remove the chicken from the marinade, reserving the marinade. Stuff the chicken with the stuffing, adding the boiled egg to the centre. Gather the legs of the chicken and tie together with a piece of kitchen string to secure the filling.

Place an ovenproof frying pan over a high heat and add the ghee. Brown the chicken on all sides until caramelised.

Now, place the chicken in a roasting tin with the remaining marinade, plus the ghee from the frying pan. Roast for 1 hour 30 minutes, or until the chicken is cooked. Regularly baste the chicken with the marinade.

Remove the chicken from the oven and carve the bird to serve with some stuffing. This is beautiful eaten with paratha or served with rice and chopped fresh coriander.

2–3 kg (4 lb 6 oz–6 lb 10 oz) whole chicken
70 g (2½ oz) Ghee (page 38)

Brine

15 g (½ oz) fennel seeds
6 g (⅛ oz) minced ginger
15 g (½ oz) whole black peppercorns
10 g (¼ oz) fine sea salt

Marinade

20 g (¾ oz) minced ginger
40 g (1½ oz) minced garlic
200 g (7 oz) hung yoghurt (see Note, page 125)
80 g (2¾ oz) almond paste (available at Indian grocers)
¼ teaspoon saffron threads, soaked in 1 teaspoon milk, then crushed to a paste

Stuffing

2 g (¹⁄₁₆ oz) green cardamom pods
10 g (¼ oz) cassia bark
40 g (1½ oz) Ghee (page 38)
150 g (5½ oz) red onion, finely sliced
500 g (1 lb 2 oz) minced (ground) chicken
10 g (¼ oz) slivered almonds
10 g (¼ oz) pistachio nuts
10 g (¼ oz) cashew nuts
10 g (¼ oz) raisins
1 hard-boiled egg, peeled
20 g (¾ oz) coriander (cilantro) sprigs, finely chopped

Utensils

Spice grinder

Sheermal

Yeasted milk bread

'Sheer' means 'milk', and 'mal' means 'knead'. This is a milk bread recipe which also uses ghee to produce a soft and decadent loaf. Sheermal recipes change according to the region. The recipe originated in Persia and is made quite differently there. Back in India, sheermal is sold on streets adjoining major mosques, and by several vendors in Delhi and Hyderabad. Some recipes drown the bread in ghee after baking, while some add the ghee beforehand. Some load the sheermal with pistachio nuts and almonds, and some make it a vibrant orange with an artificial saffron colour. All varieties of sheermal are mostly eaten with meaty, saucy and spicy dishes to mop up the liquid, and with kebabs. Here, I am sharing a basic version of sheermal, which I find very delicious.

255 ml (8½ fl oz) full-cream (whole) milk, plus extra for brushing

45 g (1½ oz) sugar

7.5 g (¼ oz) dried yeast

375 g (13 oz / 2½ cups) plain (all-purpose) flour

¾ teaspoon fine sea salt

100 g (3½ oz) Ghee (page 38), softened

Heat the milk in a saucepan over a low heat for 3 minutes, or until lukewarm. Add the sugar and stir to dissolve, then add the yeast and mix well. Remove from the heat and set aside for 10–15 minutes until bubbles begin to form on the surface.

Add the flour to the milk and bring together with your hands into a dough. Add the salt and continue kneading for 5–7 minutes.

Cover with a tea towel (dish towel) and rest at room temperature until doubled in size. Punch the dough down and shape it into a flat 20 cm (8 in) square. Spread one-quarter of the ghee on top and fold in each corner to form a smaller square. Now fold it again into a rectangle, then fold it one more time to make a square. Cover the dough with an upturned bowl and rest for 10 minutes.

Flatten the dough to a square shape again and repeat the process above another three times.

Preheat the oven to 250°C (480°F).

Cut the dough into approximately six 80 g (2¾ oz) portions and shape into balls.

Roll each ball out into a disc about 1 cm (½ in) thick. Prick the dough all over with a fork. This prevents the dough from puffing up too much in the oven.

Brush the bread with a little extra milk, place on a baking tray lined with baking paper and bake for 5 minutes, or until golden brown on top. Once cool, the bread can be stored in an airtight container at room temperature for 2–3 days.

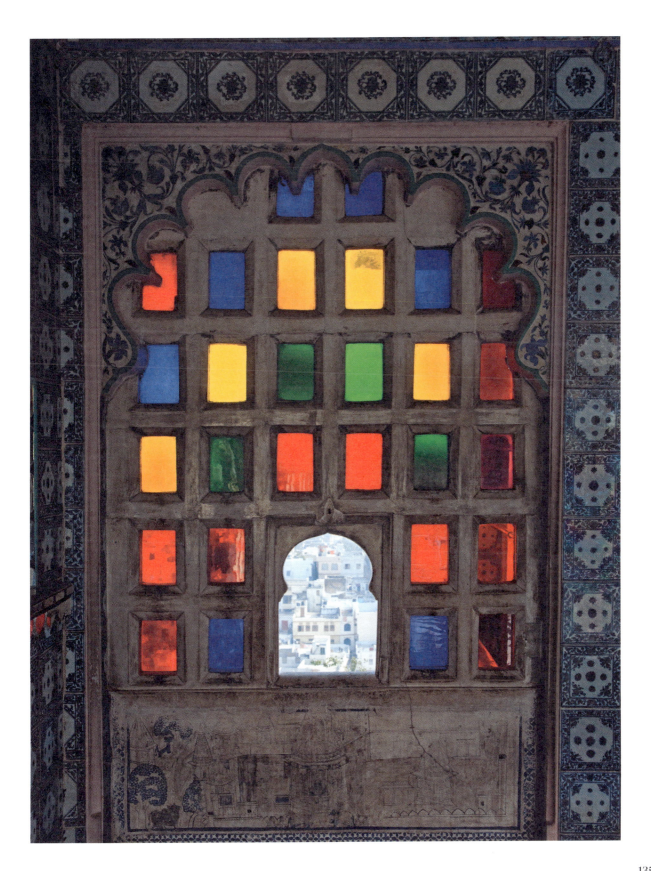

135

Naan-e-besani

Yeasted gram flour bread

The idea for this recipe stood out to me in Salma Hussain's book *The Mughal Feast*, which details popular recipes under emperor Shah Jahan's rule. This recipe is a wonderful example of how Mughal cooks incorporated native produce in their kitchens, as besan (chickpea flour) is a native grain high in protein and free of gluten. Besan is commonly used as a binder or batter to dip vegetables in before deep-frying them, or making pudla (a type of crêpe) out of thin batter, or thick, deep-fried dough. However, the use of besan to make naan, roti and paratha is seen more in north India, particularly in Delhi and Punjab. The use of ginger juice instead of crushed ginger, and replacing the usual ground coriander and green chilli with a little cinnamon, brings a beautiful depth to this naan. I have reworked this recipe to get my desired texture and replaced the slow, wild fermentation with yeast. Serve this naan with a spicy meat or poultry dish with a thick sauce, or eat it with butter for breakfast!

190 g (6½ oz) besan (chickpea flour; see Note)

1 teaspoon ground cinnamon

60 g (2 oz) Ghee (page 38), plus extra for cooking

100 g (3½ oz) plain yoghurt, at room temperature

1.5 g (¹⁄₁₆ oz) dried yeast

3 teaspoons ginger juice (made by grating fresh ginger)

75 g (2¾ oz) plain (all-purpose) flour

Utensils

Tava or flat pan

Note

Besan (chickpea flour) is essential to the recipe and cannot be replaced.

Sieve the besan and cinnamon into a bowl. Add the ghee and a pinch of salt and bring together with your hand into a stiff dough. Cover and leave to rest for 1 hour at room temperature.

Mix the yoghurt and yeast together in another bowl and let it sit for 15 minutes.

Now add the yoghurt mixture to the besan dough and knead it together. Add the ginger juice and knead well.

Add the plain flour, bit by bit, until it is all incorporated (add a little warm water if the dough is too stiff), then knead for another 10 minutes. Cover the dough and leave to rest for 1½ hours.

Divide the dough into 5 equal portions, form each portion into a smooth ball, then flatten into a disc. Roll out to make rotis about ½ cm (¼ in) thick.

Heat a dry tava or flat pan over a medium heat, add a roti and cook for 2 minutes. Flip it over and cook for another 1 minute over a medium–high heat.

Spread 1 tablespoon ghee evenly over the roti, flip again and cook until golden. Remove from the pan and repeat with the remaining dough and ghee.

Eat while hot.

Sitaphal kulfi

Frozen reduced milk with custard apple kulfi

The memory of kulfi sends me back to my hometown of
Ahmedabad, where on weekdays after dinner we would go
out for a dessert and a spicy drink called hajma hajam in the
summer. One of our favourite desserts was mango kulfi from
Ashrafi, a shop which sold several flavours of kulfi, including
sitaphal (custard apple), which had pieces of custard apple laced
through it, shaped into a cone on a stick. Kulfi is not specific
to Ahmedabad; it is found everywhere in India and more so in
the northern states. It was mentioned in *Ain-i-Akbari*, which
documented the Mughal Empire under Akbar. In Delhi, where
kulfi is said to have originated, Mughals were believed to have
brought ice from the Himalayas to Delhi to make this cold,
sweet dessert, where they laced it with rose, saffron, pistachio
nuts and mangoes.

Pour the milk into a kadhai or heavy-based wok, preferably one made
from aluminium.

Place over a medium heat and bring to the boil, stirring and scraping the
bottom to ensure it doesn't stick.

Reduce the heat a little and keep boiling until the milk reduces by
one-quarter.

Add the sugar and cardamom seeds, if using, and mix well, then simmer
for another 5 minutes over a medium heat.

Take the milk off the heat and add the custard apple. Mix well.

Pour the mixture into the kulfi mould and place wooden ice-cream sticks
in each. Attach the lid of the mould or wrap in plastic wrap and foil to
keep it airtight. Freeze overnight.

To serve, dip the mould in hot water to loosen the kulfi, then pull it out by
the stick.

1 litre (34 fl oz/4 cups) full-cream (whole) milk, at room temperature

40 g (1½ oz) sugar

2 green cardamom pods, seeds crushed to a powder (optional)

60 g (2 oz) sitaphal (custard apple), peeled and cored

Utensils

Kadhai or heavy-based wok

Kulfi mould and wooden ice-cream sticks

Falooda

Noodles, rose syrup and reduced milk

Falooda is a refreshing, cold dessert which was originally a Persian invention, made by chilling and freezing noodles, rose syrup and lemon. The Mughals, who were heavily influenced by the Persians, brought this recipe to India and made it in a much richer base. While later evolutions of the dish added ice cream, the quintessential aspects of Indian falooda remain: basil seeds, also called tukmaria, sabja or falooda seeds, as well as the noodles, milk and rose syrup. Often, rabdi – an Indian dessert made from reduced milk – and nuts are added, as well as kulfi, with a cherry on top! I am sharing a version that I imagine would have been made in the olden days.

Place the milk in a pot and bring to the boil over a medium heat, then reduce the heat to low and simmer for 10 minutes. Collect the milk skin that forms on the top with a slotted spoon and place in a bowl. Continue to repeat the process of allowing the milk skin to form and collecting it until the milk has reduced to 150–200 ml (5–7 oz). This process can take up to 1 hour.

Once the milk has reduced, add the milk skin back in, turn off the heat and add the sugar. This is your rabdi. Leave to cool to room temperature.

Bring a saucepan of water to the boil over a high heat and cook the falooda sev until soft. Drain and cool under cold running water.

To serve, place 1–2 tablespoons rose syrup in two tall glasses. Divide the falooda sev between them, then add the drained falooda seeds.

Next, add 75 g (2¾ oz) rabdi to each glass.

Add the remaining milk and garnish with the fruit and nuts, if using, and then top with crushed ice.

The kulfi can be added too for extra richness, if you like.

1 litre (34 fl oz/4 cups) full-cream (whole) milk, at room temperature

55 g (2 oz/¼ cup) sugar, plus 3 extra tablespoons

45 g (1½ oz) falooda sev (dried cornflour noodles; see Notes)

45 ml (1½ fl oz) rose syrup (see Note)

2–3 tablespoons falooda seeds (basil seeds; see Note), soaked in 250 ml (8½ fl oz/1 cup) water for 1 hour, then drained

200 g (7 oz) chopped fruit of your choice (banana or pineapple work well)

30 g (1 oz) cashew nuts (optional)

1 tablespoon pistachio nuts (optional)

crushed ice, to serve

½ stick Sitaphal kulfi, chopped (page 138; optional)

Notes

Falooda seeds (basil seeds) and rose syrup can be found at Indian grocers.

Falooda sev are dried noodles made from cornflour, and they too can be found at Indian grocers.

Kali gajjar halwa

Shredded purple carrot cooked in milk and sugar

'Kali' means 'black', and 'gajjar' means 'carrot'. This dessert is one of the simplest to make, needing only a few ingredients without cutting corners on the incredible taste. Halwa is believed to have come to India from Persia, but stories claiming a Turkish origin are popular too. Shira, or shiro, (semolina, milk and ghee cooked together) is another similar counterpart of halwa found in Gujarat too, which makes me speculate that perhaps India had its own historical version of halwa. Kali gajjar halwa is special as it uses beautiful purple carrots which make the dessert dark purple to almost black in colour.

60 g (2 oz) Ghee (page 38)

800 g (1 lb 12 oz) purple carrots, peeled and grated

2.5 litres (85 fl oz/10 cups) full-cream (whole) milk, at room temperature

180 g (6½ oz) sugar

5 g (⅛ oz) green cardamom pods, seeds crushed to a powder

1 tablespoon rosewater

8 g (¼ oz) slivered nuts of your choice

1 leaf of edible silver, to garnish

Utensils

Kadhai or heavy-based wok

Heat the ghee in a kadhai or heavy-based wok over a medium heat until hot but not smoking.

Add the grated carrot and cook for 3 minutes, stirring continuously.

Add the milk and mix well, scraping the bottom of the pan.

Slowly increase the heat to medium–high and cook the mixture for 7–10 minutes, or until it comes to a boil. Stir continuously.

Reduce the heat to medium–low and continue stirring to make sure the mix does not catch on the bottom. Keep cooking and stirring for 15 minutes, or until all the liquid is gone.

Add the sugar and ground cardamom and stir well. Cook for another 10 minutes over a low heat.

Take off the heat, add the rosewater and stir well, then garnish with the nuts and edible silver leaf.

COLONISATION

Masala chai
Tea with ginger and spices 154

Gobi achar
Spiced cauliflower pickle 156

Aloo posto
Potatoes cooked with poppy seed paste 158

Aloo paratha
Shallow-fried flatbread stuffed with
spiced potato 159

Chicken pepper fry
Chicken cooked with pepper 163

Sorpotel
Pork with saucy Kashmiri chilli and spice paste 164

Poee
Leavened bread roll with wheat bran 167

Bebinca
Custard baked in layers 171

Sandesh
Fresh cheese curds cooked with sugar 172

The first time I was introduced to my country's history was in history class at school, and what I most vividly remember from the history class covering colonisation was the story of the Jallianwala Bagh massacre. The British government had passed the *Rowlatt Act*, which gave the British police the power to arrest anyone without any reason. A crowd of unarmed protesters and pilgrims had gathered in Amritsar, Punjab, during the Baishakhi fair at Jallianwala Bagh, to peacefully protest there. The protest was to condemn the colonial government's arrest of two prominent freedom fighters, Satyapal and Dr Saifuddin Kitchlew, as well as the *Rowlatt Act*.

When Colonel Dyer, a British soldier serving in India, came to know of the gathering, he brought around 50 soldiers there and asked them to open fire on the gathering of unarmed innocents. The firing lasted for around 10 minutes, until the soldiers exhausted their ammunition, wounding 1200 and killing 379 people according to the British government (and over 1000 by other records), including women and children. The massacre enraged Indians, and stirred Mahatma Gandhi towards the non-cooperation movement.

The British initially came to India in 1608, intending to trade in Surat through the East India Company. A sea route connecting Europe with India became popular following Portuguese explorer Vasco da Gama's voyage to Calicut. Quickly, European explorers flocked to India to pursue trading, and then to acquire territory. This included the British. On the approval of Queen Elizabeth, the British created the East India Company, which was headed by merchants wishing to procure spices, indigo and cotton from India to export to Britain. Initially, the merchants were welcomed by Indian kings, and they developed trading posts across the east and west coasts of India, developing British communities in Bombay (Mumbai), Madras (Chennai) and Calcutta (Kolkata).

Quickly, the East India Company realised the divided nature of the country, and soon became involved in Indian politics, initially amassing control over Bengal and beginning their change from a trading company to a colonising empire. The East India Company

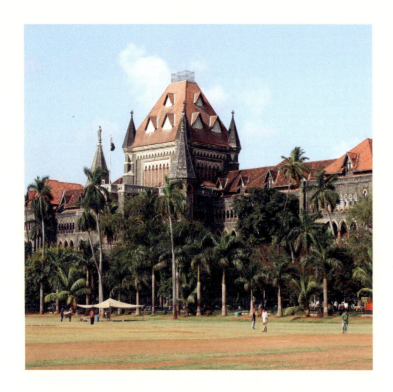

increased its control over India until the company eventually dissolved in 1858 after the Indian Rebellion of 1857, when the British Crown began to directly rule India.

The British would go on to rule India until 1947, only leaving as a result of the Indian independence movement and Mahatma Gandhi's non-violent non-cooperation movement. In 1947, India was partitioned into Muslim-majority Pakistan and Hindu-majority India, prompting one of the largest migrations in history and leading to a devastating outbreak of sectarian violence. Even as the British government passed the *Indian Independence Act* and ended their rule, they left behind a legacy of the divide they had stoked.

Britain's policies in India also led to the death of up to 29 million Indians in multiple famines, with the 1943 Bengal Famine being a prominent one in which Winston Churchill removed grain from Bengal to Britain for English soldiers, while up to 4 million Bengali people starved to death. It's not hard to see why observing and celebrating any culinary contribution by the British to India is a challenging and sensitive exercise. Much of the food of this era was influenced by the Portuguese and the ingredients they

brought with them to their colony in Goa. Some, like tomato, potato, chilli and cabbage, are now considered essential to the cuisine. The Portuguese also introduced influences from other settlements they had been in, such as South Africa and Brazil. A good example is the culture of cheesemaking from chenna (fresh cheese curds), which took Bengali confectionery by storm with the introduction of several mithai (confectionery items), like Sandesh (page 172), kalakand, chenna jalebi, cham cham, roshogolla and ras malai, which all used chenna as the base ingredient.

Bakeries in Goa were also heavily influenced by the Portuguese, and led to the creation of 'pao', or 'bread', originally 'pav' in India. Vinegar was also introduced by the Portuguese, and quickly became essential to dishes like sorpotel and vindaloo.

The British, meanwhile, brought cauliflower to India in 1822, and several types of stews were soon created using cauliflower. Dishes like aloo gobi and paratha also started being made with this vegetable. In the hands of the local people, cabbage was also cooked with spices, making it even more flavourful.

While the atrocities committed by the British were and still are the defining features of this era, the food was ever-evolving and entering a stage of multicultural fusion. The British and Portuguese officials, who missed their local foods, would get Indian cooks to make stews, cutlets, chops, roasts, puddings and lightly spiced curries, and soon the food they were familiar with was Indianised over time under the inevitable influence of the Indian cooks who made them.

The foundation of Indian cuisine had changed again, from its beginning as a means of sustenance and nourishment catering to the environment and the individual, to exploring new flavours that immigrants and traders brought, and now incorporating new ingredients from Europe. During this time, Anglo-Indian communities, which generally consisted of people with mixed Indian and British ancestry, came up with their own recipes that were neither English nor Indian, such as ball curry, yellow rice, dal bhat, jhal frezi, country captain, mulligatawny, vindaloo, chaps, cutlets, devil's chutney and puddings. British produce was adopted into the local recipes, and a milder, somewhat Indianised British food came to the fore.

Masala chai

Tea with ginger and spices

Contrary to what many might think, the popularity of tea in households across India is relatively recent. However, tea consumption in India is centuries old among some of its Indigenous groups, such as the Singpho people in Assam who are known to have drunk wild tea since the twelfth century. In the late 1600s, there were reports of tea being consumed near trade routes, but tea production in India really expanded during the colonial period when the British looked for alternative sources of tea from China, and found it in Assam. Initially, tea was produced mainly for export, with only a minority of the locals drinking it, but by the early 1900s Indian tea culture had evolved unique brewing techniques with the addition of local spices. In the 1930s, a marketing campaign which aimed to increase tea consumption in India promoted it as a healthy, patriotic beverage, and tea became associated with the Indian independence movement, cementing its place in history. Advancements in the processing of tea made it more affordable and widely spread, leading to the rise of roadside vendors of tea and popularising Indian tea-brewing styles, such as masala chai. Today, masala chai remains one of the quintessential everyday beverages of India. I, like most Indians, believe that my mum makes the best tea in the world, so here I am sharing her recipe.

Masala

25 g (1 oz) whole black peppercorns

25 g (1 oz) green cardamom pods

1–2 whole cloves

2 cm (¾ in) cassia bark stick

50 g (1¾ oz) ground ginger

Chai

½ tablespoon loose-leaf black tea

2.5 cm (1 in) piece fresh ginger, peeled and minced

200 ml (7 fl oz) full-cream (whole) milk

2 teaspoons sugar, or to taste

3–4 mint leaves

¼ teaspoon Masala (see above)

Utensils

Spice grinder

To make the masala, toast the whole spices in a dry frying pan for 5 minutes over a low heat. Remove and leave to cool completely. Grind the spices to a powder in a spice grinder, then combine with the ground ginger. Sieve if needed.

For the chai, combine the black tea, ginger and 400 ml (13½ fl oz) water in a pot. Bring to the boil over a medium heat.

Add the milk and bring it back to the boil, then reduce the heat to low and simmer for 2 minutes.

Add the sugar, mint leaves and masala and mix well, then simmer for another minute over a low heat.

Strain into a cup and drink hot.

Gobi achar

Makes 600 g (1 lb 5 oz)

Spiced cauliflower pickle

Cauliflower has been cultivated in India for the last 200 years. It was introduced from England in 1822 by Dr Jemson of Company Bagh, Saharanpur. The imported seeds were tested in various parts of India and, once it was being successfully grown, it was used for several applications, one of which is a pickle. Gobi pickle is the perfect condiment to serve with many mains, and a great way to preserve this delicate vegetable.

Place the cauliflower in a bowl, mix in the salt and leave to sit for 1 hour. Drain any water that has gathered in the bottom of the bowl, squeezing the cauliflower florets between your palms.

Lay the florets on a clean tea towel (dish towel) and air-dry for 2–3 hours.

Place the cauliflower in a mixing bowl with the garlic and chilli.

To make the dry masala, toast the fennel seeds, mustard seeds, coriander seeds, nigella seeds and fenugreek seeds in a dry frying pan over a low heat. When they start popping, take them off the heat. Add the toasted seeds to a blender with the turmeric, chilli powder and asafoetida. Blend to an almost smooth powder and set aside.

Heat the mustard oil in a saucepan over a medium heat until the oil starts to smoke, about 2 minutes.

Add 25 g (1 oz) dry masala to the oil and mix well, then immediately pour the spiced oil over the cauliflower, garlic and chilli, and mix to coat Add the vinegar, and mix again.

Check the seasoning and add some more salt if needed, then place the pickle in a sterilised glass jar (see method, page 38), seal and leave at room temperature for 3–4 days. Once fermented, store in the fridge for up to 1 week.

Serve with parathas.

800 g (1 lb 12 oz) cauliflower, cut into small florets
30 g (1 oz) fine sea salt
4 garlic cloves, peeled
2 green chillies
300 ml (10 fl oz) mustard oil
50 ml (1¾ fl oz) malt vinegar

Dry masala
1 tablespoon fennel seeds
2 tablespoons mustard seeds
2 tablespoons coriander seeds
2 tablespoons nigella seeds
1 tablespoon fenugreek seeds
1 tablespoon ground turmeric
1 tablespoon red chilli powder
2 pinches of asafoetida

Aloo posto

Potatoes cooked with poppy seed paste

Posto (white poppy seed) is a by-product of the Opium Wars of the nineteenth century. The British East India Company had found a cunning way of enslaving Bengali farmers to produce cheap opium to trade with China. As a result of this thriving, state-run global trade, exports of posto increased dramatically at the beginning of the nineteenth century, with the majority coming from India. During this time, the farmers' wives discovered the poppy seeds from the poppy seed heads or pods that remained and dried after the opium harvest. These seeds are nutty and nutritious, and food-deprived locals soon made recipes using the left-over seeds in abundance, as in this recipe of aloo posto, an indirect British contribution to Indian cuisine.

85 g (3 oz) posto (white poppy seeds), soaked in cold water for 4 hours

110 ml (4 fl oz) mustard oil

1 large onion, thinly sliced

3 dried red chillies

1 teaspoon nigella seeds

1 dried bay leaf

2 tablespoons minced ginger

1 kg (2 lb 3 oz) potatoes, peeled and cut into 2 cm (¾ in) cubes

pinch of sugar

3 green chillies, destemmed and sliced

Utensils

Kadhai or heavy-based wok

Strain the posto and blitz to a coarse paste in a blender. Add a little water to achieve the right consistency.

Heat the mustard oil in a kadhai or heavy-based wok over a medium heat until it becomes pale yellow in colour and just starts to smoke.

Add the onion and fry until golden, about 7–8 minutes, then remove it from the pan and set aside.

Keep the oil over a medium heat and add the dried red chillies, nigella seeds and bay leaf, and fry until the bay leaf pops. Add the ginger and stir well.

Add the posto paste and cook over a low heat for 3 minutes, or until the oil separates.

Add the potatoes with a pinch of salt and mix well to ensure the potato is well coated in the oil and posto paste.

Cover and cook over a low heat for 15 minutes, or until the potatoes are soft. You may need to add a little water if the potatoes start to catch.

Once cooked, add the sugar, fried onion and green chilli. Mix well without breaking the potato.

Serve with rice.

Aloo paratha

Shallow-fried flatbread stuffed with spiced potato

Aloo, or potatoes, were originally brought to India by the Portuguese, although today you will find at least a kilo of potatoes sitting in every Indian household's store cupboard. The potato is such a versatile vegetable. In Indian cooking, it is added to stir-fried vegetables to bulk up the main ingredient, mashed and stuffed into samosas, dosas and parathas, and used to make tikkis. Here, I am sharing my favourite application for aloo – the paratha. The best paratha that I've ever had was at Paranthe Wali Gali in Delhi. My recipe is an attempt to re-create what I ate there, though surely lacks the buzz of Paranthe Wali Gali and the rich theatre of its making there in the old dusty shop, which is a historic and iconic spot in itself.

250 g (9 oz/1⅔ cups) atta flour

35 g (1¼ oz/¼ cup) plain (all-purpose) flour, for dusting

50 g (1¾ oz) Ghee (page 38), for frying

1 tablespoon salted butter

Stuffing

3 medium roasting potatoes

1 teaspoon grated fresh ginger

¼ red onion, finely sliced

1 green chilli, destemmed and finely chopped

½ teaspoon coriander seeds, toasted and crushed

⅛ teaspoon caraway seeds

½ teaspoon cumin seeds, toasted and crushed

½ teaspoon amchur (dried mango powder)

¼ teaspoon Indian black salt

2–3 coriander (cilantro) sprigs, finely chopped

Add the atta flour to a bowl with a pinch of salt and 250 ml (8½ fl oz/1 cup) water. Bring together into a dough with your hands, then knead for 10 minutes. Place the dough back in the bowl, cover with a tea towel (dish towel) and rest for 30 minutes.

To make the stuffing, put the potatoes in a saucepan and cover with salted water, then bring to the boil over a high heat. Boil for 15 minutes, or until soft, then drain and leave to cool. Once cool, peel the skin and mash the potatoes in a large bowl.

Add all the remaining stuffing ingredients to the mashed potato and mix well, then season to taste with salt.

Portion the dough into 60 g (2 oz) pieces and roll them into balls.

Dust your kitchen bench with flour and roll each ball into a 10 cm (4 in) disc. Take 50 g (1¾ oz) filling and place it in the middle of a dough disc, then bring the edge of the dough together and pinch to seal the filling. Press the filled dough between the palm of your hands to flatten, then carefully roll out until the paratha is 1 cm (½ in) thick. Repeat with the remaining dough and filling.

Heat a dry, heavy-based frying pan over a medium heat and place the paratha in the pan, rolled side down. Cook for 2 minutes, then flip and cook the other side over a high heat for 1 minute.

Remove from the pan and brush about ½ tablespoon ghee on each side of the paratha. Return to the pan and cook until the blisters are crunchy and caramelised. Repeat with the remaining parathas.

Place on a serving plate and top with knobs of salted butter. Serve with yoghurt.

Chicken pepper fry

Serves 2

Chicken cooked with pepper

During colonial times, a community of Anglo Indians came into existence. This community was formed of people with mixed Indian and British ancestry, or British people who settled in India. The food they ate was different from Indian food, and dishes were adapted to suit the British palate during this time. Some were milder than the original Indian versions, which were too pungent for British taste. Pepper seemed to be a common spice in many Anglo-Indian dishes, and a preferred flavour in food. Chicken pepper fry is a good example of such dishes – simpler, and more gently spiced.

500 g (1 lb 2 oz) chicken drumsticks
10 g (¼ oz) freshly crushed black pepper
15 g (½ oz) minced garlic
15 g (½ oz) minced ginger
45 ml (1½ fl oz) vegetable oil
150 g (5½ oz) red onion, sliced
200 g (7 oz) baby potatoes, boiled
1 lime

In a bowl, combine the chicken drumsticks with the pepper, garlic, ginger and a pinch of salt. Mix well and leave to marinate in the fridge for 1 hour.

Heat the oil in a frying pan over a medium heat and add the sliced onion. Fry until translucent.

Now add the marinated chicken and cook over a high heat for 5 minutes, or until the chicken gets a bit of colour.

Now reduce the heat to low and cook the chicken for 15 minutes, stirring occasionally, and allow it to caramelise.

Add the boiled potatoes to the pan, mix well and cook for another 5 minutes.

Place the chicken and potato mix on a serving plate and enjoy with a bread roll.

Sorpotel

Pork with saucy Kashmiri chilli and spice paste

Sorpotel was brought to India from Brazil by the Portuguese. Back in Brazil, it was cooked with pig offal, blood and vinegar. However, when it landed in Goa the dish was Indianised with the addition of toddy vinegar (fermented coconut tree sap) and Kashmiri chillies instead of pig's blood, as well as spices local to the region, like pepper and cinnamon. This dish has now become one of the most popular Goan dishes, often eaten during Christmas in Goa, when it is served with bread rolls or Poee (page 167). Typically, sorpotel is made days in advance and cooked a little every day to mellow down the sharp toddy vinegar and intensify the spices.

Add all the ingredients for the spice paste to a blender and blitz to a smooth paste.

Place the pork liver and shoulder in a saucepan with the turmeric and season with salt to taste. Add enough water to submerge the meat, then bring to the boil over a high heat. Lower the heat to medium and cook for 30 minutes, or until the pork is soft and cooked through, then take off the heat.

Remove the meat from the pan and set aside on a chopping board. Allow the stock to cool to room temperature. Dice the liver and shoulder into small cubes.

Place another saucepan over a medium heat and add the oil. Once hot, add the diced onion and fry for 7 minutes, or until caramelised. Add the diced pork and fry for another 8 minutes until golden.

Turn off the heat. Leaving the oil in the pan, remove the pork and onion and set aside. Add the spice paste to the pan and return to a medium heat. Fry the paste for 7–8 minutes, stirring continuously. When the oil starts separating from the sides of the pan, return the pork and onion to the pan and stir to coat them thoroughly with the spice paste. Add the vinegar and mix well.

Now add 750 ml (25½ fl oz/3 cups) of the pork stock, season to taste with salt and mix well to coat the pork in the spice paste and oil. Add the green chillies and continue cooking for 15 minutes over a medium heat to thicken the gravy slightly.

Serve with bread rolls.

500 g (1 lb 2 oz) pork liver

500 g (1 lb 2 oz) skinless, boneless pork shoulder

10 g (¼ oz) ground turmeric

80 ml (2½ fl oz/⅓ cup) vegetable oil

230 g (8 oz) red onion, diced

200 g (7 oz) Spice paste (see below)

45 ml (1½ fl oz) malt vinegar

2–3 green chillies

Spice paste

40 g (1½ oz) red Kashmiri chillies, seeds removed, soaked in warm water for 3 hours

45 g (1½ oz) garlic cloves, peeled

10 g (¼ oz) ground turmeric

30 g (1 oz) minced ginger

6 g (⅛ oz) cassia bark

2 g (1/16 oz) whole cloves

155 ml (5 fl oz) malt vinegar

5 g (⅛ oz) black mustard seeds

7 g (⅛ oz) cumin seeds

5 g (⅛ oz) whole black peppercorns

Poee

Leavened bread roll with wheat bran

Serves 2

Poee (pronounced *poo-ee*) is a delicious bread that is eaten for breakfast, lunch and dinner in Goa. The Portuguese brought baking culture to Goa, and when I visited I found several old wood-fired bakeries that baked fresh bread twice a day. Today, the dough for this bread is usually leavened with yeast, but some traditional bakeries still use toddy vinegar, which is fermented coconut tree sap. This bread is unique, with a coating of wheat bran and a soft texture that is perfect for soaking up sauces, like in the dish Marron kodi with okra (page 208). Fresh and hot out of the oven, it is also delicious just with some cold butter and jam.

You will need to start making this recipe the day before you want to serve it.

Mix together the sugar and the lukewarm water in a small bowl. Add the yeast and mix well, then leave to sit in a warm place for 15 minutes until the yeast activates.

Mix the atta and plain flour with the salt and activated yeast in another bowl, then add the extra 200 ml (7 fl oz) lukewarm water a little at a time. Bring it together into a dough with your hands and knead for at least 10 minutes, or until you have a smooth dough.

Place the dough in a bowl and cover with plastic wrap. Leave in a warm spot for about 1 hour until doubled in size, then punch it down to knock out the air. Cover again and refrigerate overnight.

The next day, remove the dough from the fridge and let it rise until doubled in size. This can take 1 hour. Again, punch it down to knock out the air, then portion the dough into 50 g (1¾ oz) pieces and shape into smooth balls.

Dust your kitchen bench with some of the wheat bran and roll out each dough ball into a 10 cm (4 in) disc.

Place the discs on a baking tray lined with baking paper and top with a generous amount of the wheat bran. Cover with another tray, ensuring it doesn't touch the surface of the dough. Leave to prove for another 2 hours.

Preheat the oven to 250°C (480°F).

Bake the dough for 2 minutes, or until the poee puff up.

Serve with butter, if you like.

2 g (¹⁄₁₆ oz) sugar

110 ml (4 fl oz) lukewarm water, plus 200 ml (7 fl oz) extra

10 g (¼ oz) dried yeast

220 g (8 oz) atta flour

180 g (6½ oz) plain (all-purpose) flour

6 g (⅛ oz) fine sea salt

200 g (7 oz/2 cups) wheat bran

Bebinca

Custard baked in layers

Serves 4

Bebinca is a Goan dish that was invented during the period of Portuguese reign in Goa. One story says that a Portuguese nun invented this dish, which is made of a thin batter of coconut milk, egg yolks, flour, ghee and nutmeg. The thin batter is cooked in seven layers. First a layer is placed inside a pot, then covered with a lid. The lid is then topped with hot coal and coconut husk, which cooks the batter with indirect heat, resulting in a slightly charred and caramelised batter. This process is then repeated to create several distinct layers and a beautiful caramelised flavour. This dessert is popular at Christmas, and is another example of how Indian baking culture was influenced by the Portuguese. The newer evolution of this dish uses caramel, although I am sharing the original recipe here. Use freshly extracted coconut milk for the best-tasting final product.

225 g (8 oz) egg yolk

225 g (8 oz) sugar

900 ml (30½ fl oz) fresh or tinned coconut milk

225 g (8 oz/1½ cups) plain (all-purpose) flour

½ teaspoon fine sea salt

pinch of ground nutmeg

200 g (7 oz) Ghee (page 38), softened

Whisk the egg yolks in a bowl or use a stand mixer fitted with the whisk attachment and beat until pale yellow.

Gradually incorporate the sugar, a little at a time, until the mixture is pale yellow and fluffy. This will take about 12 minutes.

Fold in the coconut milk with a metal spoon until it is well combined, then fold in the flour in small batches. Add the salt and nutmeg and mix well.

Grease a 30 cm (12 in) square cake or roasting tin and line with baking paper. Preheat the oven's grill setting to 200°C (390°F).

Pour 300 g (10½ oz) of the batter into the base of the tin, place in the top of the oven underneath the grill (broiler) and bake for 7 minutes. The layer will cook and grill at the same time, making it slightly caramelised on top.

Remove the tray from the oven and then brush the baked batter with some ghee.

Pour another 300 g (10½ oz) of batter on top of this layer and bake for another 7 minutes. Brush with more ghee. Repeat this process until you have seven layers, making sure that each layer is well caramelised on top.

Remove from the oven and leave to come to room temperature, then cool in the fridge for 3 hours.

Once set, slice the bebinca into either squares or rectangles – whatever you prefer.

To serve, warm it up in the oven or microwave and serve with ice cream, sorbet, baked fruit, compote, or fresh fruit of your choice.

Sandesh

Fresh cheese curds cooked with sugar

Chenna, also known as paneer, is believed to have been eaten since pre-Vedic times, although its popularity declined during the Vedic era when the Aryans worshipped cows. Central Asians also prepared paneer and introduced it to the subcontinent, but its popularity shot up when the Portuguese brought it to Bengal in the seventeenth century, with Bengalis preparing several sweet dishes out of chenna. As well as being used in sweet preparations, paneer is now a popular addition to savoury recipes, and is often used as a replacement for meat. Here, I am making sandesh, a sweet made from chenna with saffron.

2 litres (68 fl oz/8 cups) full-cream (whole) milk

200 g (7 oz) plain yoghurt

approx. 75 g (2¾ oz) icing (confectioners') sugar (see Note)

pinch of saffron threads

1 teaspoon slivered pistachio nuts (optional)

Note

The yield of the chenna can vary. The amount of sugar used should be 10 per cent of the weight of the chenna yield (or a little more or less depending on your taste).

Pour the milk into a saucepan and simmer over a medium heat until it reaches 75°C (165°F) on a cooking thermometer. Add the yoghurt and stir gently. The milk will start separating and become clear.

Strain the whey and reserve the milk solids – this is your chenna.

Cool the chenna slightly, then, while it is still warm, knead it on your kitchen bench for 10 minutes with pressure until you have a smooth cheese. Add the sugar and knead until fully incorporated.

Heat a frying pan over a low heat and cook the chenna for 7 minutes, spreading it out to cook it evenly. Be careful not to discolour the mixture.

Remove from the pan and leave until cool enough to handle, then knead for another 5 minutes.

Roll the sandesh into 15 g (½ oz) balls and press between the palms of your hands to create thick discs. Use your thumb to make a small indent in the middle of each disc.

Crush the saffron threads to a powder with a mortar and pestle. Add a few drops of water and mix well.

Brush the saffron paste in the indents of some of the sandesh and place some slivered pistachio nuts on top of the others, if using.

MODERN INDIA

It is the beginning of a new era for India. Our future shines bright with the knowledge that our strong foundations, laid thousands of years ago, stand as evidence we are and have long been an enlightened and holistic civilisation. We have a rich cultural, intellectual and culinary heritage that extends back to ancient times, and the legacy we carry forward is invaluable. Now is an age of restoring the knowledge that was destroyed, misunderstood and belittled. The modern world has only recently started understanding and discovering practices mastered in ancient India long ago. Indians worldwide are curious to understand and discover their heritage. We no longer look to the West for direction or validation. The self-doubt seeded by colonisation and invasion is in retreat, and we look towards unity and peace to sustain us in the future. The perception of Indian culture and food is changing.

In this modern era, the West has continually undermined the value of developing countries. This has had a major impact on food, food habits and the environment in developing countries: policies and manipulative practices have affected what we produce and what we eat. Loans from the World Trade Organization and World Bank have allowed rich countries and agricultural giants to prevent the storage of seeds, introduce genetically modified crops, and use pharmaceutical drugs and pesticides that have damaged the land and entered the ecosystem.

The damage to traditional local food production and consumption has been substantial. The trend towards modern eating habits continues apace and interest in hyper-local produce has shrunk – processed cheese and poor-quality mayonnaise are now commonly served with dosa and dabeli on the streets of India. While there is no harm in growing new produce in India, like avocados for avocado toast and milkshakes (both now popular street foods), there needs to be equal or greater importance given to restoring near-extinct native, sustainable heirloom produce.

From my frequent visits back home, I am still hopeful we might strike a balance. We haven't yet commercialised the majority of our food items and habits in India, and desi (old-fashioned food) still exists in many households. We prefer to buy fruits and vegetables from our local vendors instead of supermarkets; we still store grains once a year when they're in season; and we still source spices from our trusted suppliers. Turmeric and ghee are still used for healing, and Ayurveda continues to be practised in the modern world. When we feel under the weather only khichdi will do, and we use wholemeal (whole-wheat) flour, not refined. Ghar ka khana, a home-cooked meal, is still considered the best.

A rediscovery of Indian cooking is coming to the fore. It incorporates the techniques, cultures, ingredients and recipes from the past that make us who we are. Today, many chefs back home take pride in bringing their heritage into the limelight through restored produce and cooking techniques. There is no better time to be an aspirational Indian chef with strong values and a passion for serving diners hungry for purpose, reclamation and pride.

In my kitchen here in Australia I am continually inspired by Bhartiya cuisine. I aspire to cook with the nourishment prescribed in the Vedic era. Seasonality and sustainability are at the heart of what I make. I use seafood that is native to Australia, choose vegetables that are in season and meats that are local. I take inspiration from the openness to novelty and experimentation that was prominent during the era of trade and migration, while using Australian produce to create regional Indian dishes. From the Mughal era, we learned to evolve our cuisine while maintaining authenticity by trying to find the soul of a recipe and keeping it unchanged. My cooking today is deeply informed by the knowledge I have learnt and now shared with you in this book.

I dearly miss my produce from back home, but in this new home away from home we are blessed with exceptional produce too. Native Australian produce has been used by the Traditional Custodians of the land I live on, the First Nations People whose country was colonised, since time immemorial. Yet the delicious, nourishing and medicinal applications are still unknown to many.

Though more sustainable to produce, these products and processes have not gained enough popularity to replace the mainstream produce brought over by colonisation and migration. I apply my curiosity and the principle of using local and seasonal ingredients, and find hints of amla in native lemon aspen. I find the sweet sourness of tamarind in Davidson plums, and the creaminess of cashew in macadamia. The sourness of desi lime is indistinguishable from that of desert lime. Yes, nothing can replace turmeric, but the fragrant floral notes and numbing peppiness of native Tasmanian mountain pepper is just as unique and irreplaceable. Saffron production is rare here, though the fragrance that leatherwood honey can add to a mithai is no less than that of the most expensive spice on earth.

In spring during Diwali, my family in Melbourne and I often hunt for morels in the Macedon Ranges to make Bharwa gucchi pulao (page 207). We knock on neighbours' doors for beautiful magnolia flowers to pickle for months to come, and during the summer holidays we treasure picking beach herbs, and getting the first of the eggplants (aubergines) and heirloom tomatoes. The end of summer is special too, when fresh pistachios come in for just a few weeks, whereas in autumn we get on the saffron milk cap–picking bandwagon with all the chefs and enthusiastic cooks in Victoria who look for this beautiful orange fungi. We covet the smoky, creamy and delicious tuber Jerusalem artichoke that appears at the same time, which I use to make bharta (mash; see page 206). Come winter, yuzu and truffles are on everyone's mind. There is no way you cannot use the exceptional produce that this land has to offer, incorporating what your background has taught you and what you as a cook want to create.

In this last chapter I share with you the recipes I cook at my restaurant, Enter Via Laundry in Melbourne. The produce might be native and seasonal but the soul of the recipe stays Bhartiya.

Heirloom radish pickle

Makes 1 kg (2 lb 3 oz)

Pickles are a quintessential Indian condiment. I love the fermented sourness that a pickle brings to the plate, acting almost like a palate cleanser. Whether it is roti, vegetables, dal, rice or meat, eating a mouthful of pickle halfway through always adds a boost of flavour. Growing up in my mother's home, asking for more pickles during a meal was considered rude, as it implied that the items on the thali (a large plate containing a variety of foods) were not delicious enough on their own! For me, at times, this pickle does indeed become a main instead of a condiment.

To make the spice mix, toast the whole spices in a dry frying pan over a low heat for 5 minutes, then cool to room temperature. Blitz to an almost-fine powder in a spice grinder. Mix in the turmeric and chilli powder.

Wash the radishes and pat dry with paper towel. Leave to air-dry on a clean tea towel (dish towel) for 2 hours. Slice any large radishes in half lengthways and leave the smaller ones whole.

Place the radishes in a large, heatproof mixing bowl and add the salt, sugar and vinegar. Mix well.

Heat the oil in a small saucepan over a low heat and add the spice mix, garlic cloves and green chillies. Heat for about 2 minutes, or until the oil is hot but not smoking, then tip the hot oil over the radishes and mix well.

Transfer the radishes and oil to a sterilised glass jar (see method, page 38). Secure a piece of cloth over the mouth of the jar and tie with kitchen string. Place the lid loosely on top. Leave for 4–5 days at room temperature to ferment the radish. Give it a good stir every day to mix the liquids and spices. Taste the pickle every day to check the flavour, too – you want a pickle that's a little sour but still crunchy.

Once ready, transfer it to the fridge and store for up to 3 weeks.

I like to eat this pickle with fluffy rice and ghee with some pickle juice, radish and a green chilli.

1 kg (2 lb 3 oz) heirloom rainbow radishes, greens removed
40 g (1½ oz) fine sea salt
10 g (¼ oz) sugar
40 ml (1¼ fl oz) apple-cider vinegar
150 ml (5 fl oz) sunflower oil (see Note)
25 g (1 oz) Spice mix (see below)
20 g (¾ oz) garlic cloves, peeled
6 whole fresh green bird's eye chillies

Spice mix
25 g (1 oz) red mustard seeds
25 g (1 oz) coriander seeds
25 g (1 oz) nigella seeds
12 g (¼ oz) fennel seeds
10 g (¼ oz) fenugreek seeds
1 teaspoon ground turmeric
1 teaspoon red chilli powder

Utensils
Spice grinder

Note
Generally, back home, we use cottonseed oil when we need an odourless oil, but it isn't widely available – not even in Indian grocers – so I tend to use sunflower or vegetable oil in its place.

Native citrus preserve

Makes 1.1 kg (2 lb 7 oz)

Each country has its own native citrus. Naarm (Melbourne), where I have my restaurant, has its own, and I believe we have some of the best varieties in the world, with truly unique flavours, shapes, fragrances and textures. The finger lime has citrus juice encased in tiny pearls, blood limes are tear drop–shaped, and tiny desert limes have even tinier bubbles inside filled with citrus juice that reminds me of Indian lime. The sunrise lime has this bright yellow and orange tinge and is slightly numbing on the tongue if eaten whole. All of these citrus fruits have edible, thin, flavourful skin, which is almost always utilised in recipes. This recipe is a simple pickle that uses all these varieties of native Australian citrus, though it can be made with simple lemons and limes, too.

200 g (7 oz) finger limes
300 g (10½ oz) blood limes, halved
300 g (10½ oz) desert limes
300 g (10½ oz) sunrise limes
4 g (⅛ oz) ground cumin
5 g (⅛ oz) ground turmeric
10 g (¼ oz) red chilli powder
300 g (10½ oz) caster (superfine) sugar

Wash and dry all the limes. Cut the finger limes into 1 cm (½ in) slices, and halve the sunrise limes lengthways.

Mix the cumin, turmeric and chilli powder in a large mixing bowl with the sugar and salt to taste. Add the limes and mix well.

Place the mixture in a sterilised glass jar (see method, page 38). Secure a piece of cloth over the mouth of the jar and tie with kitchen string. Place the lid loosely on top.

Leave in the sun to macerate and ferment for 5 days. Stir the mixture every day to coat the limes with the sugar and spice mix.

Test your pickle after 5 days and if the skin of the limes is still tough, you may need to ferment it for another day or two.

This pickle will keep in the fridge for up to 2 weeks once opened.

Marron head rassam

Spicy and sour broth with marron head

They say there is nothing a rassam cannot cure. Like ghee in the North, the South is obsessed with this preparation. The original recipe included pepper, a few spices and tamarind. Now, it incorporates the pepperiness and sourness of tamarind with chilli, turmeric and coriander (cilantro). Once, when we had some left-over marron heads, we added them to this rassam – the flavour blew us away. This dish evolved from that joyful discovery. The sweet, delicate flesh of the marron tail is beautiful in a sauce (see Marron kodi with okra, page 208), while the head meat can be used in stocks and broths – in this case a rassam.

To prepare your marron, start by bringing a large pot of water to the boil. Fill a large bowl with iced water.

Drop the marron into the boiling water and cook for 1 minute, then take them out and immediately plunge into the iced water.

Remove the heads and claws from the tails by twisting with your hands.

Using scissors, cut along the back of the tail shells on the soft side, keeping the tails intact (you can use the tail flesh in Marron kodi with okra, page 208). Remove and discard the digestive tract and shell.

For the masala paste, toast the cumin, coriander and fenugreek seeds in a dry frying pan set over a low heat for 5–10 minutes. Remove and leave to cool.

Add the toasted seeds to a mortar with the garlic, coriander roots and black pepper, and pound to a smooth paste. Add some salt to help create the right consistency.

Place the marron heads in a pot with 3 litres (101 fl oz/12 cups) water, the turmeric, red chilli powder and a pinch of salt (not too much, as the stock will reduce and become saltier).

Add the masala paste and cherry tomato and bring the stock to the boil over a high heat. Cook for 10 minutes, then reduce the heat to low and cook for another 12 minutes, or until the liquid has reduced to about 2 litres (68 fl oz/8 cups).

Remove the marron heads and discard.

Now make the tadka. Melt the ghee in a saucepan over a high heat. When the ghee is hot, quickly add the urad dal, followed by the mustard seeds, asafoetida, red chilli and curry leaves. Pour the hot oil and spices into the rassam and cook over a low heat for another 5 minutes.

Add the jaggery, and taste and adjust the seasoning. Garnish with fresh coriander, if using, and serve with rice.

4 small marron heads with claws, or king prawns (shrimp)

1½ teaspoons ground turmeric

¼ teaspoon red chilli powder

350 g (12½ oz) cherry tomatoes, halved

5 g (⅛ oz) jaggery

finely chopped coriander (cilantro), to garnish (optional)

Masala paste

3 g (⅒ oz) cumin seeds

12 g (¼ oz) coriander seeds

3 g (⅒ oz) fenugreek seeds

10 medium-sized garlic cloves, peeled

30 g (1 oz) coriander (cilantro) sprigs, roots separated

10 g (¼ oz) whole black peppercorns

Tadka

10 g (¼ oz) Ghee (page 38)

3 g (⅒ oz) urad dal

3 g (⅒ oz) red mustard seeds

3 pinches of asafoetida

2 dried red chillies, halved

1 curry leaf sprig, leaves picked

Parindey shorba

Bird bone broth with warm spices

This recipe was featured on our Mughaliya menu in the winter of 2023. Its ingredients are a by-product of another recipe, parindey musallam, a Mughaliya dish made by deboning a bird and stuffing it with another bird as well as eggs. For this dish, we use a whole duck, chicken and quail. This recipe uses poultry bones, though it can be made with other animal bones as well. It is a warming recipe that uses the same spices as a Nadru yakhni (page 127), although here the spices are toasted instead. It can be served as a soup before the start of a meal, or with some shredded chicken and vegetables as a whole meal. Here, I am sharing the recipe for the basic broth.

Preheat the oven to 180°C (360°F). Combine all the whole spices in a bowl and set aside.

Place all the bird bones in a roasting tin and drizzle the vegetable oil and salt on top. Toss to combine.

Sprinkle the ginger and garlic on top, followed by the sliced onion and leek.

Roast the bones for 45 minutes, or until well caramelised, then take the tin out, add the whole spices and return to the oven for another 10–15 minutes, being careful that the spices don't burn.

Remove the bones and spices from the tin and place in a large ovenproof stockpot that will fit inside your oven. Add enough water to fully submerge the bones.

Cover the pot and place in the oven, reduce the heat to 120°C (250°F) and cook for 2 hours. Remove the pot from the oven and leave to come to room temperature.

Strain the stock into a clean saucepan. If it's a little cloudy, you can strain it through a piece of muslin (cheesecloth) to get a nice clear broth.

To serve, heat the stock in the saucepan and season to taste. It will keep in the fridge for up to 4 days or the freezer for 4 weeks. Serve as a soup with bread on a cold day.

20 whole cloves
5 g (⅛ oz) whole black peppercorns
3 g (⅒ oz) cassia bark
3 g (⅒ oz) black cardamom pods
1 g (1⁄32 oz) green cardamom pods
5 g (⅛ oz) fennel seeds
bones from 1 duck (see Note)
bones from 1 chicken (see Note)
bones from 3 quail (see Note)
2 tablespoons vegetable oil
1 tablespoon fine sea salt, plus extra to taste
10 g (¼ oz) piece fresh ginger, peeled and crushed
15 g (½ oz) garlic cloves, crushed
1 onion, sliced
½ leek, roughly chopped

Note
Ask your butcher for fresh bird carcasses for this recipe.

Lemon myrtle nankhatai

Makes 20–22

Sweet teatime biscuits

Nankhatai are nostalgic treats I cherish. Crumbly, buttery and sweet, they're made with ghee, a blend of flour and sugar, and a herb or spice flavouring. Enjoyed with tea or on their own, nankhatai are believed to have originated in Surat, Gujarat, with Dutch, Iranian and local culinary influences. Gujarati bakeries make nankhatai with cardamom, rose, saffron and pistachio flavours, but this recipe uses lemon myrtle, a fresh, lemony sweet herb native to Australia. Gujarat has a predominantly vegetarian population, and so nankhatai are made without eggs. Different flours are used to achieve a crumbly texture, and the besan (chickpea flour) holds the ingredients together in place of protein.

In a large bowl, whisk the ghee and sugar together until the mixture is pale yellow in colour.

Sift the maida flour, then the besan, into the ghee and sugar mixture. Add the sooji, lemon myrtle and salt.

Use a spatula to gently fold the dry ingredients into the ghee and sugar mixture, until the ingredients are well incorporated. Take care not to overmix the dough.

Cover with a tea towel (dish towel) and set the dough aside in a cool place to rest for 15 minutes.

Roll the dough into balls, each one approximately 40 g (1½ oz), and place on a baking tray lined with baking paper. Refrigerate the dough balls for 20 minutes.

Preheat the oven to 140°C (285°F).

Bake the dough balls in the oven for 20 minutes, rotating the tray after 10 minutes to ensure an even bake.

Remove from the oven and allow to cool completely before transferring the nankhatai to a cooling rack.

230 g (8 oz) Ghee (page 38); room temperature, not melted

235 g (8½ oz) caster (superfine) sugar

260 g (9 oz) maida flour or plain (all-purpose) flour (see Notes)

120 g (4½ oz) fine besan (chickpea flour)

60 g (2 oz) sooji (fine semolina; see Notes)

5 g (⅛ oz) ground lemon myrtle (see Notes)

3 g (⅒ oz) fine sea salt

Notes

Maida flour can be found at Indian grocers, as can sooji, which is a fine semolina. Italian semolina will not work well with this recipe.

You can substitute lemon myrtle with rose petals, lemon verbena, cardamom or another flavour of your choice. (Just adjust the amount you use depending on the intensity of the herb or spice.)

Mango chutney with cinnamon myrtle

Serves 4

No matter how elaborate our meals might be, there is always a special place for chutneys in Indian cuisine. Chutneys go on samosas and kebabs, are eaten with rice and breads, and sometimes halfway through a mouthful of biryani, rice and sabji a lick of chutney is added to bring an electric dash of flavour. In my household we always make several fresh chutneys that are then frozen to keep enjoying throughout the year. This particular recipe celebrates mangoes. I have also added red chilli and cinnamon myrtle, which is a native Australian herb.

200 g (7 oz) ripe mango flesh, diced

4 g (⅛ oz) fine sea salt

1 red chilli, destemmed and finely chopped

1 cinnamon myrtle sprig, leaves stripped (available from suppliers of native Australian ingredients)

Place the mango in a bowl and add the salt, chilli and cinnamon myrtle leaves. Mix well.

Transfer the mixture to a 200 ml (7 fl oz) sterilised glass jar (see method, page 38) and seal with the lid (you can also use a vacuum-sealed bag here).

Leave the jar in a warm spot for 3–4 days, or until the chutney starts to ferment. If you're using a jar, open and re-seal the lid a couple of times a day to let out the gas and avoid an explosion.

Once the mango mixture is fermented, place it in a blender and blitz to a smooth paste. Return to a sterilised glass jar and store in the fridge for up to 1 week.

Truffled dum aloo

Serves 2

Baby potatoes cooked in yoghurt and truffle

Every part of India has a dum aloo recipe, but what's interesting is that none of the recipes actually use 'dum', or steaming, as a method to cook the potatoes, although it is still called dum aloo! Recipes differ from Kashmir to Punjab to Bengal, and I cook it differently here in Australia, too. I'll be honest: come truffle season I am in search of a dish that can incorporate truffles and let them be the highlight, and this dum aloo recipe is an invention born out of my passion for winter truffles. They have an unmatchable earthy flavour, and their aroma is one of my favourite smells. It immediately transports me to a dense, quiet forest.

Soak the garlic in 2 tablespoons water and set aside.

Add the fried shallot to a blender with 3 tablespoons water and blitz to a smooth paste.

Bring a saucepan of salted water to the boil and boil the potatoes for 10–12 minutes, or until almost cooked and still holding their shape. Drain, leave to cool to room temperature, then peel.

Drain and discard the garlic, reserving the water.

Heat the oil in a frying pan over a medium heat and add the cardamom and clove. Now add ½ teaspoon of the reserved garlic water, trying to avoid making the oil sputter. Repeat the process, adding more garlic water until it has all been used. Now add the fried onion paste and mix well.

Add the mountain and white pepper and mix well, then add the sour cream and shaved truffle, stirring continuously.

Add the black salt, followed by the peeled potatoes and mix gently to avoid breaking them. Remove from the heat and garnish with the extra shaved truffle and native oregano leaves.

Eat with a puri (deep-fried wholemeal bread) or Bhatura (page 229).

2 garlic cloves, minced

4 small shallots, thinly sliced and deep-fried (see Note, page 121)

250 g (9 oz) baby potatoes

60 ml (2 fl oz/¼ cup) vegetable oil

2 green cardamom pods

2 whole cloves

½ teaspoon mountain pepper (available from suppliers of native Australian ingredients; see Notes)

½ teaspoon ground white pepper

200 g (7 oz) sour cream

10 g (¼ oz) fresh black truffles, plus extra to garnish

¼ teaspoon Indian black salt

10 native oregano leaves, to garnish (see Notes)

Note

A combination of black pepper and sichuan pepper can be used instead of mountain pepper.

I use Australian native oregano (*Prostanthera rotundifolia*) as a garnish, but you can use coriander instead.

Paperbark undhiyu

Serves 4

Smoky vegetables with coriander marinade

I used to make this recipe at my home restaurant in Box Hill, Melbourne. Undhiyu is a regional recipe from Surat, Gujarat. It is made in winter when root vegetables are plentiful and vanaspati (a wild weed that imparts a smoky aroma when cooked) grows. Root vegetables are marinated with coriander (cilantro), garlic, ginger, green chilli and caraway seeds. An earthenware pot is first lined with vanaspati, then the vegetables are placed inside it. The pot is sealed and covered with lots of dry grass, hay and wood, which is then set on fire. After an hour or so the pot is removed from the fire and left to cool. The smoky vegetables are then served with a tart chutney made of a local fruit called kotha, and some sesame oil. Here, I am making an Australian version of this recipe with local ingredients: the bark from a paperbark tree for smokiness and tart Davidson plums for the chutney. It's the perfect marriage of Gujarati culture and Australian produce.

Prepare a coal-fuelled barbecue. Tip a bag of charcoal into the barbecue. Place 3–4 barbecue fire starters at equal intervals in the barbecue and light them. Fan the coals to encourage flames. Once the fire has caught, cover half the barbecue with a lid to encourage all the coals to catch alight.

Combine all the marinade ingredients in a blender and blitz to a smooth paste.

Add the root vegetables and the marinade to a large bowl, and mix well. Leave to marinate for 2–3 hours.

Use the paperbark to line an earthenware pot big enough to hold all the vegetables, then place the veg inside and seal the pot tightly with aluminium foil. Place the pot directly on hot barbecue coals, cover and cook for 45 minutes, or until the vegetables are soft.

To make the chutney, put the plums in a saucepan with the sugar, 200 ml (7 fl oz) water and a pinch of salt. Bring to a simmer over a medium heat and cook for 15 minutes.

Remove from the heat and let it come to room temperature. Once cool, blitz in a blender or with an electric mixer until smooth, adding a little water if necessary to loosen.

To serve, plate the vegetables and dot with the Davidson plum chutney. This can be enjoyed as a side or a light lunch with roti.

250 g (9 oz) jicama, cut into bite-sized pieces

250 g (9 oz) baby potatoes, halved

250 g (9 oz) purple potatoes, cut into 4 cm (1½ in) cubes

250 g (9 oz) sweet potatoes, cut into 4 cm (1½ in) cubes

Marinade

1½ bunches of coriander (cilantro)

200 ml (7 fl oz) peanut oil

20 g (¾ oz) garlic cloves

15 g (½ oz) piece fresh ginger, peeled

1 teaspoon ground turmeric

3 green chillies, destemmed

1 tablespoon sugar

¼ teaspoon carom seeds

juice of 1 lemon

Davidson plum chutney

250 g (9 oz) Davidson plums, pips removed

250 g (9 oz) sugar

Utensils

Charcoal, for smoking (see Note)

Paperbark, to line your earthenware pot (available from suppliers of native Australian ingredients; see Note)

2 litre (68 fl oz/8 cup) earthenware pot

Note

Wood chips can be used to smoke undhiyu if charcoal is not available, and banana leaves can be used to line the earthenware pot in place of paperbark. Banana leaves are available at Asian grocers.

Patra nasturtium poda

Prawns marinated with coconut and charred nasturtium leaf

'Patra' refers to leaves, and 'poda' means burnt. There is a fascination in the fine-dining scene with the nasturtium plant. You will often see it included in oils, dusts and intricate plating that uses numerous small leaves. I have tried all of these things with nasturtium, so the only thing left to experiment with was to burn it. This Odia dish is traditionally made with pumpkin (squash) leaves and makes a perfect vehicle for burnt nasturtium! The marinade needs next to no preparation too, making this a fantastic barbecue party dish. We served it as one of our entrées at Enter Via Laundry and it was a winner.

Blitz the marinade ingredients in a blender with 1 teaspoon water to form a paste.

Tip into a bowl with the prawns, mix well, and place in the fridge to marinate for at least 30 minutes.

Remove the prawns from the marinade and wrap each prawn individually in a nasturtium leaf. Place on a tray.

Grill the prawns over a medium heat for 3–4 minutes, or until cooked. Squeeze the lime juice over the top.

Thread two prawns onto a skewer and place on a plate. Repeat with the remaining prawns and skewers, and serve as an entrée.

350 g (12½ oz) small prawns (shrimp)

1 medium nasturtium leaf per prawn (see Note)

juice of 1 lime

Marinade

60 g (2 oz) coconut powder (available at Indian grocers)

50 ml (1¾ fl oz) mustard oil

5 g (⅛ oz) minced garlic

2 g (1/16 oz) finely diced green chilli

5 g (⅛ oz) sugar

Utensils

Wooden skewers

Note

You can use pumpkin (squash) leaves or even bok choy leaves instead of nasturtium leaves.

Khandavi

Serves 4

Gram flour ribbons with coconut sauce

Khandavi is the dish that marked the beginning of my journey. This dish gave me the courage to do what I do now. I know every chef and cook talks about food from childhood, but there is some magic when you cook something you loved in childhood. Perhaps childhood is the most defining phase of life, and hence when revisited with love it brings so much acceptance and joy! Regardless, this dish is tasty, and its silky delicious ribbons have always made me happy. This typical besan (chickpea flour) preparation is generally eaten as a snack, but at Enter Via Laundry I make it look a little fancy. I called the dish 'I am not pasta', as I was so bored of pasta being one of the most popular foods in Melbourne. Calling my dish 'not pasta' attracted so much attention that I don't know if I am sad or happy about it. But the dish is delicious, and so I want to share my original version of 'I am not pasta' with you.

220 g (8 oz/2 cups) besan (chickpea flour)

1½ teaspoons ground turmeric

2 pinches of asafoetida

edible flower petals or coriander (cilantro) leaves, to garnish (optional)

Thai basil oil

1 bunch Thai basil

185 ml (6 fl oz/¾ cup) vegetable oil, plus extra for greasing

Lemongrass and red chilli oil

20 g (¾ oz) red chilli powder

185 ml (6 fl oz/¾ cup) vegetable oil

4 lemongrass stalks, trimmed

Tempered coconut sauce

15 ml (½ fl oz) vegetable oil

2 pinches of asafoetida

5 g (⅛ oz) mustard seeds

5 g (⅛ oz) sesame seeds

1 green chilli

2.5 cm (1 in) piece fresh ginger, peeled and finely chopped

400 ml (13½ fl oz) tinned coconut milk

1 tablespoon sugar

To make the Thai basil oil, briefly blanch the basil leaves in boiling water, then immediately refresh in an ice bath. Drain and blend with the oil, then pass this mixture through a clean disposable cloth or muslin (cheesecloth) and collect the oil.

For the lemongrass and red chilli oil, add the chilli powder to the oil in a saucepan and heat it to 50°C (120°F) on a cooking thermometer. Remove from the heat and leave to cool a little, then strain through a clean disposable cloth or muslin and collect the oil.

Combine the oil with the lemongrass in a blender, and blitz until smooth. Pass this oil through another clean disposable cloth or muslin and collect the oil.

Make the khandavi by mixing the besan, a pinch of salt, turmeric and asafoetida with 1 litre (34 fl oz/4 cups) water. Use an electric mixer to blend into a smooth batter, then strain into a jug.

Lightly rub the base and side of a pot with oil and pour in the besan mixture. Clean your kitchen bench and rub it with a little oil, too.

Cook the besan mixture over a low heat for 7 minutes. Increase the heat to medium and continue cooking, scraping the bottom continuously with a spoon. When the mixture starts to thicken, switch to a whisk and continue stirring – it can take up to 30 minutes to reach the right consistency (the batter will turn glossy and thick and form laces).

Use a dough scraper to evenly spread the batter onto your greased benchtop to 3 mm (⅛ in) thick. Cut it into strips about 5 cm (2 in) wide. Roll these strips up and set aside.

To make the coconut sauce, heat the oil in a saucepan over a medium heat, then add the asafoetida, mustard seeds, sesame seeds and green chilli. Once the mustard seeds start to pop, add the ginger and coconut milk and boil for 4–5 minutes, then add the sugar and season with salt, stir well, then remove from the heat.

Unfurl two to three ribbons of khandavi on each serving plate. Pile them high, then pour the sauce over the top. Drizzle with both oils, then garnish with the edible flower petals or coriander leaves, if using.

Jerusalem artichoke bhorta cooked in whey with Tasmanian mountain pepper

Bhorta is a quintessential Bengali dish, although other parts of India have similar dishes called bharta. The original concept of the recipe, coming from the Bengali dish aloo bhorta, uses potatoes, but at Enter Via Laundry, we use one of my favourite vegetables – Jerusalem artichoke. It has a smoky, earthy flavour that works perfectly in winter recipes. This bhorta could be eaten with rice and dal, with a whole green chilli on the side for a kick! You could even spread it on a piece of toast and add some beautiful blue cheese on top.

To make the whey, combine the milk and yoghurt in a saucepan and bring to a simmer over a medium heat. Cook until the milk solids separate and the whey is clear. Strain the whey through a fine-mesh sieve. Reserve the milk solids to make chenna (see page 223), or ricotta. Left-over whey will keep in the fridge for up to 3 days and can be used to make bhatura dough (see page 229).

Peel the Jerusalem artichokes, reserving the peel, then cut the artichokes and potatoes into bite-sized pieces and place in a saucepan with the whey.

Bring to the boil over a high heat, then reduce the heat to low and simmer until soft and starting to caramelise. All the whey should evaporate; this can take up to 1 hour. Stir regularly to prevent the potatoes from sticking. Season with the white and mountain pepper, and some salt to taste.

Heat 100 g (3½ oz) of the butter in a frying pan and fry the onion until caramelised, about 8 minutes.

Add the caramelised onion, garlic and remaining butter to the artichoke and potatoes and mash together well.

Wash the artichoke peel.

Heat enough oil for deep-frying in a saucepan until it reaches 180°C (360°F) and deep-fry the peel for 3 minutes until crunchy. Drain on paper towel.

Garnish the bhorta with the crispy peel at the last minute. Serve with rice and dal.

1.5 litres (51 fl oz/6 cups) whey (see below)
1.5 kg (3 lb 5 oz) Jerusalem artichokes
500 g (1 lb 2 oz) roasting potatoes, peeled
1 teaspoon ground white pepper
½ teaspoon ground mountain pepper (available from suppliers of native Australian ingredients; see Note), or to taste
150 g (5½ oz) butter
1½ red onions, finely sliced
2 large garlic cloves, finely chopped
vegetable oil, for deep-frying

Whey

3 litres (101 fl oz/12 cups) full-cream (whole) milk
600 g (1 lb 5 oz) plain yoghurt

Note

A combination of black pepper and sichuan pepper can be used instead of mountain pepper.

Bharwa gucchi pulao

Rice cooked with Kashmiri spices, wild garlic and stuffed morels

I am not a fan of getting tattoos, but if I ever get one, it will be of wild garlic, also known as three-cornered garlic. Why? Because it is as delicious as garlic but also looks exceptionally beautiful: tiny garlic bulbs in the root system, garlicky green leaves and beautiful white garlic flowers. I love to combine this winter and early spring produce with morel mushrooms. I use the entire wild garlic plant in my gucchi pulao. The word 'gucchi' means 'morels', and it is special to find the same produce here in Melbourne, and to use it in a traditional Kashmiri recipe.

Wash the rice once, then drain and set aside. If you're using dried morels, soak them in 250 ml (8½ fl oz/1 cup) water to rehydrate.

Heat the ghee in a frying pan over a medium heat and toast the whole spices for 30 seconds.

Add the onion, garlic stems and garlic bulbs, and cook for 8 minutes, or until they turn golden.

Drain the morels and reserve the soaking liquid.

Take one-third of the hydrated morels, slice them and add to the onion.

Add the turmeric, Kashmiri chilli powder and a pinch of salt, stir well and cook for 1 minute.

Add the rice and mix until all the grains are evenly coated in the spices.

Add 375 ml (12½ fl oz/1½ cups) of the water used to soak the morels, and mix everything well. Check and adjust the seasoning.

Add the fennel and ground ginger and stir well. Cook for 5–6 minutes over a medium heat. Stir gently, then cover and cook for 5–7 minutes, or until the rice is cooked but not mushy. Remove from the heat.

To make the stuffing, combine all the ingredients in a bowl and mix well. Stuff the remaining morels with the mixture and set aside.

Heat the oil in a shallow frying pan and fry the stuffed morels for 2 minutes, or until cooked. Season to taste with salt and pepper.

Transfer the pulao to a serving plate and place the stuffed morels on top. Garnish with the mint and garlic flowers, and serve with yoghurt.

250 g (9 oz) basmati rice

10 large dried or fresh morel mushrooms (see Notes)

35 g (1¼ oz) Ghee (page 38)

2 small bay leaves

1 g (1/32 oz) star anise

5 green cardamom pods

1 large black cardamom pod

½ cassia bark stick

150 g (5½ oz) onion, diced

20 g (¾ oz) wild garlic, stems finely chopped, flowers reserved for garnish (see Notes)

10 g (¼ oz) wild garlic bulbs, washed and cleaned (see Notes)

3 g (1/10 oz) ground turmeric

3 g (1/10 oz) Kashmiri chilli powder

5 g (1/8 oz) ground fennel seeds

2 g (1/16 oz) ground ginger

2 tablespoons vegetable oil

1 mint sprig

Stuffing

80 g (2¾ oz) paneer, grated

15 g (½ oz) khoya (dried evaporated milk solids; see Notes)

½ teaspoon crushed black peppercorns

1 small green chilli

1 teaspoon lime juice

1 shallot, finely diced

Notes

If you replace the morels with another mushroom just make sure they have cavities big enough to hold the stuffing.

Garlic chives can be used if wild garlic is not available.

Khoya is available from an Indian grocer.

Marron kodi with okra

Serves 4

This Goan recipe is a delicate preparation of coconut, mild spices, tomatoes and prawns (shrimp). In a humble Konkani bungalow in south Goa, a local lady named Philomena invited us to a traditional Goan meal and made us this Sungta bhenyachi kodi, that is prawn and okra kodi. It was delicate, delicious and satisfying. I wasn't sure if it was the freshness of the ingredients, the honest setting, the love of this lady who was very inviting or all of it that made this one of the most special meals I have ever had. Here in Melbourne during our Goan menu in 2023 we made this dish to go with red rice and marron head ghee (both are excellent accompaniments). This recipe uses prawn heads to bring flavour to the sauce, and marron tail for its beautiful sweetness and texture.

Drain the soaked Kashmiri chillies and set aside.

Heat a dry frying pan over a medium heat and toast the cumin and coriander seeds for about 6 minutes, then set aside.

Combine the garlic, 35 g (1¼ oz) diced shallot, tomatoes, toasted seeds and Kashmiri chillies in a blender and blitz to a smooth paste. Now add the coconut and its soaking water and the 3 g (⅛ oz) of the turmeric and blend everything together. Strain the mixture through a fine-mesh sieve into a saucepan.

Set the saucepan over a low heat and cook for 8 minutes, stirring continuously.

Add the prawn heads and cook for another 8–10 minutes. Add some water if the mixture starts to reduce too much (it should be a pouring consistency).

Strain the mix into a clean saucepan and add the remaining shallot, the green chillies and okra. Bring to the boil over a medium–high heat and cook for 5 minutes. Add a little water if it begins to reduce too much – this is not a thick sauce. Season to taste then take off the heat.

To process the marron, start by bringing a large pot of water to the boil. Fill a large bowl with iced water.

Drop the marron into the boiling water and cook for 1 minute, then take them out and immediately plunge into the iced water.

Remove the heads by twisting them off with your hands, followed by the claws.

Using scissors, cut along the back of the tail shells on the soft side, keeping the tails intact. Remove the digestive tract and shell. Toss the marron in the remaining turmeric and a pinch of salt.

6–10 dried Kashmiri chillies, soaked in cold water overnight

4 g (⅛ oz) cumin seeds

10 g (¼ oz) coriander seeds

8 g (¼ oz) garlic cloves

70 g (2½ oz) shallots, peeled and diced

150 g (5½ oz) tomatoes, roughly diced

850 g (1 lb 14 oz) freshly grated coconut, soaked in 1.4 litres (47 fl oz) water

3 g (⅒ oz) ground turmeric, plus ½ teaspoon extra

4–5 banana prawn (shrimp) heads

3 green chillies

80 g (2¾ oz) bhinda (okra; see Notes)

6 × 120–150 g (4½–5½ oz) marron (see Notes)

knob of butter

Notes

King prawns (shrimp) can be used instead of marron. You may like to reserve the marron heads for Marron head rassam (page 190).

If you dislike the sliminess of okra, you can deep-fry it beforehand.

If you have a sous-vide machine, seal the marron in a vacuum-pack bag with a knob of butter. Bring the water temperature to 75°C (165°F) and cook the marron in the water for 5 minutes. If you don't have a sous-vide machine, poach the marron tails in the sauce for 5 minutes over a medium–low heat.

Place the marron on a serving plate (you may like to cut it into 1 cm/½ in slices), then pour the hot kodi with okra over the top and serve immediately.

Abalone with tomato and lemon gum broth

Serves 4

I came up with this dish for my restaurant's summer Goan menu. I wanted to take inspiration from Salada De Cavalas Salgadas, a fresh salad from Goa which is made with salted mackerel, tomatoes, coriander (cilantro) and onions. The end product that started with this inspiration, however, became dramatically different – the tomatoes became a broth, abalone replaced the mackerel and lemon gum replaced the coriander. This dish quickly became one of the most loved on the menu!

You will need to start the broth 1 day in advance.

Place all the broth ingredients in a blender with a pinch of salt and blitz to a smooth paste. Pour into a plastic container. Seal the container and freeze overnight.

The next day, take the frozen tomato and coconut block out of the container, place it on a piece of muslin (cheesecloth) set inside a strainer and place over a pot to collect the consommé.

Once all the broth is collected and the entire block of tomato and coconut water has defrosted, transfer the broth to a jar, season to taste and keep cool in the fridge. Discard any solids.

To clean the abalone, remove the meat from the shell in one piece with a paring knife, then use a small brush to clean any impurities off the circular lip of the abalone. Remove any waste from the waste organs located at the pointy end of the abalone.

Add the abalone to a vacuum-seal bag with the lemon gum, coconut water, vinegar, green chillies, sugar and a pinch of salt. Seal and cook in a sous-vide machine, if you have one, at 65°C (150°F) for 35 minutes.

If you don't have a sous-vide machine, mix everything in a pot with 250 ml (8½ fl oz/1 cup) water. Place a cartouche on the surface of the mixture and cover the pot with a lid. Cook over a low heat for 35–40 minutes, or until the abalone is soft.

Once cooked, take the abalone out and let it come to room temperature. Thinly slice the abalone and transfer to a serving plate. Pour over 120 ml (4 fl oz) of the chilled tomato and coconut broth, then garnish with the seablite, if using, and cherry tomatoes and serve immediately.

420 g (15 oz) abalone

10 g (¼ oz) lemon gum (available from suppliers of native Australian ingredients; see Note)

200 ml (7 fl oz) coconut water

100 ml (3½ fl oz) apple-cider vinegar

3 green chillies

25 g (1 oz) sugar

3 sprigs seablite (available from suppliers of native Australian ingredients), to garnish (optional)

10 cherry tomatoes, quartered, to garnish

Broth

1 kg (2 lb 3 oz) tomatoes, destemmed

200 ml (7 fl oz) coconut water

2–3 g (¹⁄₁₆–¹⁄₁₀ oz) hot green chilli

200 ml (7 fl oz) apple-cider vinegar

5 g (⅛ oz) lemon gum (see Note)

Note

Lemongrass can be used instead of lemon gum.

Masoor dal with native enoki

Red lentil dal with mushrooms

Serves 4

The word 'dal' in India refers to dried split pulses as well as the soupy nourishing dish that is made from it. Dal is one of the most comforting dishes in our cuisine, as well as one of the most humble and homely ones. There are a number of varieties of dal, but here I have one of the most ancient – masoor dal, or red lentil, that I have made with a Bengali tadka (tempering) and added some Australian native enoki mushrooms. This recipe is great without the addition of mushrooms, and it can be enjoyed with rice, Bhatura (page 229) or Pathiri (page 100).

Wash the masoor dal three or four times, then place in a bowl, cover with fresh water and soak for 3 hours.

After 3 hours, drain the masoor dal and combine in a saucepan with the turmeric, a large pinch of salt and 600 ml (20½ fl oz) water. Cook over a medium heat for 20 minutes, or until the dal is soft and cooked, stirring periodically. Top up with more water if it begins to dry out.

To another small saucepan, add the mustard oil and heat over a medium heat until it starts to smoke. Add the nigella seeds and let them pop for 10 seconds, then add the ginger and green chillies and stir well.

Add the bay leaf, then pour the contents into the cooked dal and mix well. Adjust the seasoning by adding sugar and salt to taste.

Heat the vegetable oil in a frying pan over medium heat. When the oil is hot, add the enoki mushrooms and cook until both sides are lightly browned. Season with salt to taste.

Add the dal to a serving plate and top with the enoki mushrooms. Garnish with oregano to serve.

250 g (9 oz/1 cup) masoor dal (red lentils)
3 g (1/10 oz) ground turmeric
40 ml (1¼ fl oz) mustard oil
5 g (1/8 oz) nigella seeds
20 g (¾ oz) minced ginger
2 green chillies, slit lengthways
1 bay leaf
2 tablespoons vegetable oil
200 g (7 oz) native Australian enoki mushrooms, or enoki mushrooms
native oregano, leaves stripped, to garnish (optional; see Note)

Note

I use Australian native oregano (*Prostanthera rotundifolia*) as a garnish, but you can use coriander instead.

Dohneiiong with mountain pepper, desert lime and charred warrigal greens

Serves 4

Dohneiiong is a dish from Meghalaya, a state in the north-east of India inhabited by several mountain tribes. Food here is very different from most other regions in India as the produce is very distinctive. It is one of the most richly biodiverse regions, and the locals enjoy preserved meats and hyper-regional vegetation. This dish is a specialty of the Khasi tribe, where pork – one of the more popular meats – is cooked with black sesame seeds, which are considered to have warming properties. I like to serve this with native Australian ingredients, like desert lime for a sour counterbalance, and warrigal greens for freshness.

Toast the black sesame seeds in a dry frying pan over a medium heat for 1–2 minutes.

Add the seeds to a blender with a dash of water, blend to a paste, then set aside.

Fill a large stockpot with salted water, add 2 g (1⁄16 oz) of the turmeric and the pork belly and shoulder and bring to the boil. Reduce the heat to medium and simmer gently for 25 minutes, or until the pork is soft and fully cooked. Remove the pork and let it cool to room temperature, then dice into bite-sized cubes. Reserve the stock.

In a large, heavy-based saucepan, heat the mustard oil over a high heat until it smokes.

Add the finely chopped onion and cook until translucent, then add the garlic and ginger and sauté for a few seconds. Add the remaining turmeric and cook for a further 2 minutes.

Add the sesame paste and cook for 2 minutes. Add 125 ml (4 fl oz/1⁄2 cup) of the pork stock and cook for 5 minutes. Now add the diced pork and another 125 ml (4 fl oz/1⁄2 cup) pork stock and season to taste.

Add the mountain pepper, black pepper and green chilli and mix well. Cook for another 5 minutes, topping up with a little more stock if it starts to reduce too much, then remove from the heat.

Meanwhile, rub the warrigal green leaves with oil and season with salt and pepper. Char the leaves briefly over an open flame (an open fire is ideal, but you can use a gas flame, too). Set aside.

Transfer the pork to a serving dish and dot it with the desert lime. Scatter the warrigal greens over the top and serve with rice.

60 g (2 oz) black sesame seeds

7 g (1⁄4 oz) ground turmeric

500 g (1 lb 2 oz) piece of skinless pork belly

500 g (1 lb 2 oz) boneless pork shoulder

100 ml (3½ fl oz) mustard oil, plus extra for rubbing

300 g (10½ oz) red onion, minced

30 g (1 oz) garlic cloves, minced

20 g (¾ oz) piece fresh ginger, peeled and minced

2 g (1⁄16 oz) ground mountain pepper (available from suppliers of native Australian ingredients; see Notes)

5 g (1⁄8 oz) ground black pepper

1 green chilli, destemmed and finely chopped

5–6 warrigal greens sprigs, leaves stripped (see Notes)

10–12 preserved whole desert limes (available from suppliers of native Australian ingredients; see Notes)

Notes

A combination of black pepper and sichuan pepper can be used instead of mountain pepper. Spinach can be used instead of warrigal greens, and a wedge of preserved lemon can be used instead of the desert limes.

Game pasanda

Pan-fried smoked kangaroo with floral spices

Serves 2

Pasanda is a popular dish prepared by flattening meat with a meat mallet, marinating it, and then cooking it with spices. Pasanda is a Mughaliya recipe which uses the best cuts of meat, hence the name 'pasanda' meaning 'favourite'. Originally, pasanda was a preparation with less sauce, however current local recipes contain a lot of sauce. This version is closer to the authentic original dish in its technique. I've found that kangaroo striploin works well for this preparation, and I serve it with parsnip, rose and riberries, as well as a kangaroo tail sauce.

Preheat the oven to 120°C (250°F).

To make the garam masala, toast all the spices in a dry frying pan over a low heat for 7–8 minutes. Take off the heat and leave to cool, then grind to a fine powder in a spice grinder.

Next, make the kangaroo tail sauce. Heat the ghee in a large cast-iron pot over a high heat.

Once hot, add the kangaroo tail and caramelise on all sides, then add all the remaining ingredients, except the shallot paste, and cook for 10 minutes until the leek takes on a bit of colour. Remove from the heat.

Add 500 ml (17 fl oz/2 cups) water to the pot, cover and transfer to the oven. Cook for 4 hours.

Remove from the oven and strain the broth through a fine-mesh sieve into a clean saucepan. (The kangaroo tail can be enjoyed as a meal on its own.) Add the shallot paste and place over a medium heat. Simmer for 10 minutes to reduce the broth to a buttermilk consistency. Season to taste.

Flatten the striploin with a meat mallet until it is 5 mm (¼ in) thin.

Combine all the ingredients for the marinade in a bowl. Add the striploin to a deep roasting tin and cover with the marinade.

Next, we want to smoke the kangaroo. Make a little bowl with a piece of aluminium foil and place it in the tray with the kangaroo. Add the shredded paperbark to the bowl and light it. Pour the ghee on top to create smoke. Once the flame dies down, quickly cover the tray with another piece of foil and leave to smoke for 15 minutes.

Preheat the oven to 150°C (300°F).

400 g (14 oz) kangaroo striploin (see Notes, overleaf)
2 tablespoons Ghee (page 38)
1 leaf of edible silver, to garnish

Garam masala
75 g (2¾ oz) whole black peppercorns
20 g (¾ oz) cinnamon stick
25 g (1 oz) black cardamom pods
50 g (1¾ oz) green cardamom pods
75 g (2¾ oz) whole cloves

Kangaroo tail sauce
10 g (¼ oz) Ghee (page 38)
200 g (7 oz) kangaroo tail (see Notes, overleaf)
3 garlic cloves, crushed
2.5 cm (1 in) piece fresh ginger, peeled and crushed
1 leek, roughly chopped
1 teaspoon Garam masala (see below)
1 teaspoon whole black peppercorns
1 deep-fried shallot blended into a paste with a little water (see Note, page 121)

Marinade
25 ml (¾ fl oz) pineapple juice
100 g (3½ oz) sour cream
1 teaspoon Garam masala (see above)
2 teaspoons ground coriander
15 g (½ oz) minced ginger
25 g (1 oz) minced garlic

Smoking
paperbark (available from suppliers of native Australian ingredients), shredded
30 g (1 oz) Ghee (page 38)

Continued next page →

To make the parsnip purée, place the parsnip in a roasting tin with the milk, bay leaf, white pepper and salt, to taste. Cover with foil and bake for 15–20 minutes, or until the parsnip is soft.

Remove the bay leaf, transfer the mixture to a blender and blitz to a smooth paste. Add the butter, rosewater, vinegar and sugar and blend again to incorporate.

To prepare the riberries, make a sugar syrup by combining the sugar with 50 ml (1¾ fl oz) water in a saucepan. Bring to the boil over a high heat, stirring to dissolve the sugar. Add the riberries and continue boiling for 5 minutes, then remove from the heat and leave to cool. Once cooled, these riberries can be stored in the syrup in an airtight container in the fridge for up to 4 weeks.

Now, to cook the kangaroo striploin, heat the ghee in a frying pan over a high heat until smoking. Add the striploin and cook for 30 seconds on each side. Divide the striploin into two pieces and place on serving plates.

Reheat the parsnip purée briefly on the stove, then place a dollop beside the kangaroo. Garnish with the riberries. Reheat the kangaroo tail sauce on the stove, then drizzle 2 tablespoons sauce over each piece of striploin and garnish with edible silver.

Parsnip purée

200 g (7 oz) parsnip, diced
400 ml (13½ fl oz) full-cream (whole) milk
1 fresh bay leaf
2 g (1⁄16 oz) ground white pepper
50 g (1¾ oz) butter
½ tablespoon rosewater
5 ml (⅛ fl oz) apple-cider vinegar
5 g (⅛ oz) caster sugar

Riberries

50 g (1¾ oz) sugar
25 g (1 oz) riberries (see Notes)

Utensils

Spice grinder

Notes

Any red meat can be used instead of kangaroo and plums can be used instead of riberries.

Chenna poda

Serves 4

Baked fresh cheese with figs and lemon myrtle

This sweet dish from Orissa is a relative newcomer to the Indian culinary world. The story goes that a halwai (pastry chef) left a pot of milk curds dusted with sugar on top of the diminishing wood fire, called 'chulha', and the next day he came back to find this beautiful dish that was crispy on the outside and soft on the inside. I like to make my version of it with lemon myrtle leaves and desert lime and sweet figs, and have it with some hot coffee or serve it warm with whipped sour cream for dessert.

Place the milk in a large pot over a medium heat and warm until it reaches 70°C (160°F) on a cooking thermometer.

Add the yoghurt and stir gently. The milk solids will begin to separate from the whey, and once the whey is clear, remove from the heat and strain the mixture through a piece of muslin (cheesecloth), reserving 200 ml (7 fl oz) of the whey.

Preheat the oven to 150°C (300°F).

Place the milk solids in a bowl with the ghee, jaggery and reserved whey. Add the semolina and mix well, then mix in the lemon zest, desert lime and fig.

Grease a round 20 cm (8 in) baking tin and line it with the banana leaf (to make banana leaf pliable, heat it over an open flame) and lemon myrtle leaves, then pour in the batter.

Bake for 30 minutes, increasing the heat to 200°C (390°F) for the last 6 minutes. Remove from the oven and leave to cool to room temperature before serving.

4 litres (135 fl oz/16 cups) full-cream (whole) milk, at room temperature

80 g (2¾ oz) plain yoghurt

100 g (3½ oz) Ghee (page 38)

220 g (8 oz) jaggery, grated

60 g (2 oz) fine semolina

zest of 1 lemon

30 g (1 oz) fresh desert lime (available from suppliers of native Australian ingredients)

3 fresh figs, chopped

1 large banana leaf (available at Asian grocers)

4 fresh lemon myrtle leaves (see Note)

Note

You can replace the lemon myrtle leaves with any flavourful edible leaf, such as lemon leaves.

Samphire paratha

Serves 4–5

Flatbread with samphire

Back home in Gujarat, young girls would do vrat (a fast), something which has recently come out of fashion, though my cousin and I looked forward to this time of year as the last day of the fasting was an all-night party called 'jagran', where all the cousins would gather and stay up playing cards and other games. During this vrat, we were given a special diet free of salt, onion, garlic and certain grains and vegetables. To be honest, it seemed more like a cleansing fast. The highlight during this fast was samphire, which my aunt would gather and use as a replacement for salt. My mother would also make paratha with it. At the time, we were just surprised to taste this sea succulent that appeared once a year, and when I came to Melbourne kitchens and saw samphire being used as a micro herb, I was instantly reminded of the parathas.

100 g (3½ oz) samphire (see Note)

500 g (1 lb 2 oz/3⅓ cups) atta flour, plus extra for dusting

1 teaspoon freshly ground black pepper

⅛ teaspoon carom seeds, lightly crushed between your palms

30 g (1 oz) Ghee (page 38), for frying

Note

Any salty sea herb, like seablite, sea grapes or beach bananas would work here too. Or you could replace with spinach, dill or spring onion (scallion) – they just wouldn't need to be boiled.

Bring a saucepan of water to the boil over a high heat and boil the samphire for 5 minutes, or until soft. Remove the samphire stems and chop the rest finely.

Combine the atta, samphire, pepper and carom seeds with 400 ml (13½ fl oz) water in a bowl. Bring the mixture together into a dough and knead for 7 minutes, then leave to rest for 1 hour.

Take 40 g (1½ oz) pieces of the dough and shape into smooth balls.

Dust your kitchen bench with flour and roll the balls out to 10 cm (4 in) wide discs.

Heat a heavy-based frying pan over a medium heat. Place a paratha, rolled side down, in the pan and cook for 1 minute, then flip, increase the heat to high and cook for another 40 seconds.

Add 1 teaspoon ghee to the surface of the paratha and flip it again, pressing down with a spatula as the paratha balloons up. Fry for 1–2 minutes until golden brown, then spread some more ghee on the surface and remove from the pan. Repeat with the remaining parathas.

You may like to serve these with some yoghurt and honey.

Bhatura

Deep-fried leavened bread

Bhatura is a popular deep-fried sourdough bread from the Punjab region, which is eaten with savoury gravy dishes. While the traditional recipes use yoghurt as a starter, I like making bhatura with leftover whey from making shrikhand. The whey acts as a natural yeast and brings subtle acidity and moisture to the bread. When fried, bhatura is crunchy on the outside and soft on the inside. Serve this with chutneys, Aloo posto (page 158), dum aloo (see page 197), or even with Mango chutney with cinnamon myrtle (page 196), and it's sure to be a hit!

600 g (1 lb 5 oz/4 cups) plain (all-purpose) flour, plus extra for dusting

500 ml (17 fl oz/2 cups) whey (see page 206), or 250 g (9 oz/1 cup) yoghurt mixed with 250 ml (8½ fl oz/1 cup) cold water

100 g (3½ oz) fine semolina

100 g (3½ oz) Ghee (page 38)

1 litre (34 fl oz/4 cups) vegetable oil, for deep-frying

Place the plain flour and a pinch of salt in a bowl and mix well.

Add 250 ml (8½ fl oz/1 cup) of the whey and bring the mixture together into a dough.

Start kneading, gradually adding the remaining whey to form a smooth dough. Knead for 10 minutes.

Place the dough in a deep bowl, cover with a tea towel (dish towel) and leave in a warm place for 4–5 hours.

Now add the semolina and ghee to the dough and knead until fully incorporated. Return to the bowl and leave to prove for 2 hours.

Heat the oil for deep-frying in a large saucepan until it reaches 200°C (390°F) on a cooking thermometer.

Remove the dough and divide into 50 g (1¾ oz) balls. Roll into 1 cm (½ in) thick discs with a rolling pin, dusting with flour as needed.

Drop the rolled bhatura into the hot oil and, with help of a slotted spoon, gently hold the bhatura under the oil as it starts floating up. This will help the bhatura to puff up. Fry on one side for 30 seconds, or until light golden, then flip and cook on the other side for another 45 seconds.

Take the bhatura out delicately to keep it puffed and drain the excess oil on a paper towel. Eat while warm.

Blood orange, quince and riberry pudding with strawberry gum custard

This warm pudding is a delicious winter dessert, inspired by India's colonial era and the Christian communities in India who celebrate Christmas with puddings. This dessert also celebrates the use of native Australian spices. I find riberries share a very similar spice profile to cardamom, and in this recipe I use strawberry gum in the custard instead of vanilla to add a nuanced flavour. Blood orange and quince are both great winter fruits in Melbourne, and they bring earthiness and tartness to this dessert.

Cream the butter and sugar together in a large mixing bowl with an electric mixer, or in a stand mixer fitted with the whisk attachment, until pale and fluffy. Add the eggs, one at a time, mixing to incorporate between each addition.

Fold in the lemon and blood orange zest and juice, the blood orange segments, mashed quince, and the riberries. Mix well.

Sieve the flour, cinnamon, cloves and nutmeg into a bowl, then gently fold this into the wet ingredients.

Grease a conical cake tin and pour the golden syrup into the base of the tin.

Spoon the batter into the tin and cover with foil. Steam for 1 hour using the double-boiler method. Simply set a colander over a large saucepan of simmering water, place the tin inside (taking care to make sure the tin does not touch the water), cover with foil and steam for 1 hour. Remove from the heat.

For the custard, pour the milk and cream into a saucepan, add the strawberry gum leaves and bring it to a very gentle simmer over a low heat. Remove from the heat and strain to remove the gum leaves.

In a bowl, whisk the egg yolks and sugar until pale, then gradually add the milk and cream mixture, whisking continuously.

Return this mixture to a clean saucepan set over a low heat and stir continuously with a wooden spoon while the custard thickens. Cook for 10 minutes, or until the custard coats the back of the spoon. If you run a finger through it, you should be left with a clean line and the custard shouldn't flow back in. Remove from the heat, cover the pan with plastic wrap and transfer to the fridge to cool.

Drizzle the warm pudding with golden syrup and serve with the custard.

175 g (6 oz) unsalted butter, softened, plus a little extra for greasing

175 g (6 oz) light muscovado sugar

3 eggs, beaten

zest and juice of 1 lemon

2 blood oranges, 1 juiced and zested, 1 cut into segments

150 g (5½ oz) quince, diced and poached then mashed

20 g (¾ oz) riberries (see Notes)

150 g (5½ oz/1 cup) self-raising flour

½ teaspoon ground cinnamon

¼ teaspoon ground cloves

⅛ teaspoon ground nutmeg

3 tablespoons golden syrup, plus extra for drizzling

Custard

150 ml (5 fl oz) full-cream (whole) milk

250 ml (8½ fl oz/1 cup) thick (double/heavy) cream

10 g (¼ oz) dried strawberry gum leaves (see Notes)

3 egg yolks

50 g (1¾ oz) sugar

Notes

Riberries can be replaced by plums, or any local berry of your choice. Strawberry gum can be replaced by cardamom.

Rose shrikhand, fermented blueberries and lace cookies

Serves 2

Shrikhand is a rather simple dessert in Indian cooking. It is essentially a sweetened hung yoghurt with added flavours and nuts. For Gujaratis, it is a special thali dessert (a large plate containing a variety of foods); no Gujarati thali is complete without a dollop. In summer, it is often loaded with fresh mango, and in winter it is topped with badam (almond), pista (pistachio nut) and kesar (saffron) – a holy trinity of dessert flavourings and always a crowd favourite. I enjoy these flavours dearly, but I wanted to experiment with a new flavour in fermented sour berries, the essence of rose and the crunch of lace cookies.

You will need to start this recipe 2–4 days in advance.

To ferment the blueberries, wash and pat them dry with paper towel, then add to a vacuum-seal bag with the salt and leave at room temperature to ferment for 2–4 days (depending on the temperature – the warmer the climate, the faster fermentation will occur), or until the bag fills with air. Decant into a sterilised glass jar (see method, page 38) and refrigerate.

For the rose dust, wash the rose petals and pat dry with paper towel. Place them in a dehydrator and dehydrate overnight. Once dried, blitz to a fine powder in a blender.

For the shrikhand, add the yoghurt and sugar to a bowl and whisk well. Place a fine-mesh sieve lined with a piece of muslin (cheesecloth) over a bowl. Add the yoghurt mixture and transfer to the fridge to drain overnight.

Preheat the oven to 160°C (320°F).

For the lace cookies, heat the butter, brown sugar and milk in a saucepan over a medium–low heat until the sugar has melted and the mixture just comes to the boil.

Remove from the heat and add the vanilla extract, flour, ground almonds and a pinch of salt. Stir until completely combined, then allow to cool for about 5 minutes.

Line two baking trays with baking paper and place tablespoons of cookie dough on the trays, spaced well apart to allow for spreading.

Bake for 7–10 minutes, or until the cookies are golden in colour. Remove from the oven and leave to come to room temperature, then break into shards. Store in an airtight container.

Fermented blueberries
100 g (3½ oz/⅔ cup) blueberries
10 g (¼ oz) sea salt

Rose dust (see Note)
petals from 4 large, perfumed roses

Shrikhand
750 g (1 lb 11 oz/3 cups) full-fat (whole) yoghurt
60 g (2 oz/½ cup) icing (confectioners') sugar

Lace cookies
80 g (2¾ oz) unsalted butter
125 g (4½ oz/⅔ cup) brown sugar
2 tablespoons full-cream (whole) milk
1 teaspoon vanilla extract
50 g (1¾ oz/⅓ cup) plain (all-purpose) flour
55 g (2 oz/½ cup) ground almonds

Utensils
Vacuum-seal bag

Note
You can use store-bought dried rose petals if you don't want to dehydrate your own. Dried rose is available from Indian grocers and some supermarkets.

The next day, whisk the shrikhand again – it should be stiff and creamy, and the whey should have collected in the bowl underneath. Transfer the shrikhand to a piping (icing) bag fitted with a large star nozzle.

To serve, pipe the shrikhand into serving glasses in a mound about 4 cm (1½ in) tall. Dust the rose petal powder on top using a fine-mesh sieve, then carefully arrange about five fermented blueberries on top of each. Finally, garnish with shards of lace cookie.

Yuzu lassi

In winters I always look forward to yuzu, the magnificent citrus that originated in China and was introduced to Japan and Korea by the Tang Dynasty. I love the unique fragrance of this fruit, and using yuzu in the kitchen has become a form of aromatherapy for me. In my restaurant, we used to make a palate cleanser using yuzu and yoghurt – a twist on the sweet lassi we find in Indian restaurants, but replacing the mangoes with yuzu. This beautiful yuzu lassi always features bubbles and foam, which is a technique my father taught me while making lassi at home.

250 g (9 oz/1 cup) plain yoghurt

2 tablespoons sour cream

125 ml (4 fl oz/½ cup) full-cream (whole) milk

2 teaspoons sugar, or to taste

2–3 teaspoons fresh yuzu juice

zest of ½ yuzu

10 g (¼ oz) Geraldton wax leaves

1 tablespoon macadamia oil

Mix the yoghurt, sour cream, milk and sugar in a bowl and blitz with a hand-held blender until the sugar has dissolved. Taste and adjust the sugar at this point if you would like it a little sweeter.

While blending, bring the hand-held blender almost to the surface and angle it to create bubbles.

Now add the yuzu juice and zest and mix well.

Pour the lassi into chilled glasses and garnish with Geraldton wax leaves and a few drops of macadamia oil.

Cook's notes

This book uses 250 ml (8½ fl oz) cup measurements and 15 ml (½ fl oz) tablespoons.

In the US, a cup is 8 fl oz (240 ml), just smaller; American cooks should be generous in their cup measurements. In the UK, a cup is 9½ fl oz (284 ml); British cooks should be scant with their cup measurements.

Oven temperatures in this book are fan-forced. If using a conventional oven, increase the temperature by 20°C (70°F).

Utensils and cooking methods

Appa chatti

a small clay or cast-iron round-bottom bowl for making appam

Baghar

the base of a recipe that includes hot oil and spices, followed by meat, vegetables or pulses

Bhuna

to slow roast, or slowly caramelise, ingredients in a pan with or without water

Dhungar

the process of smoking a dish with a piece of hot coal. The coal is placed in a prepared dish then covered with spices. Ghee is then poured on top to create the smoke before the whole dish is covered with a lid.

Dosa tava

a flat cast-iron pan with no sides used for making dosa

Handi

a copper pot with a narrow neck and a wide top and bottom designed to trap steam and encourage slow cooking

Kadhai

similar to a wok, but made with thicker metal, usually iron, cast iron or aluminium, or earthenware or clay

Mathani

a churner, usually made of wood

Palta

a square spatula used for flipping parathas, dosas and even scraping and mixing vegetable and meat preparations cooked in kadhai and handis

Patili

a round-bottomed pot that improves heat distribution, which helps prevent the contents from burning

Sil batta

a heavy rectangular or circular stone used for grinding

Tadka

oil tempering that is added to a cooked dish, such as dal

Tavetha

a turning spoon that is square in shape

Vaghariyu

a small, half sphere–shaped metal utensil with or without a handle that is used for tempering

Ingredients

Cassia bark

Cassia bark, or dar chini, is often preferred over cinnamon for its strong sweet fragrance.

Chilli

There is a variety of chillies in India, and they are used in many different ways: dehydrated, powdered, flaked, fresh, etc. The green chillies used in this book are Indian green chillies, or green bird's eye chillies, for their freshness and heat. Avoid using the big, dark-green cayenne chillies as these are not suited to Indian dishes. I also do not encourage taking the seeds out. If you prefer a milder heat, leave the chillies out or add a smaller quantity of Indian green or bird's eye chilli.

Dal

Urad and chana dal are slow roasted in ghee or oil as a part of tempering in south Indian dishes, which adds another dimension of texture.

Dals should always be soaked for a minimum of 1 hour and ideally 3 hours before cooking (if not roasting).

Jaggery

Jaggery is made from sugarcane juice (sugar in its raw form). It is widely available, but if you're having trouble finding it visit an Indian grocer.

Mustard

Mustard can be used in three forms: fermented, soaked and ground into a paste, or popped in oil for tadkas and baghars.

Oils

Oils play a very important role in Indian cooking. Just as mustard oil won't work for spaghetti aglio e olio, olive oil won't work for dal tadka. Acceptable oils and fats are mustard oil, sesame oil, peanut oil, sunflower oil, ghee, coconut oil, vegetable oil or canola oil.

Rice

Except for basmati, rice should be soaked for 1 hour before cooking.

Saffron

In my household, we never use saffron threads until they are crushed and dissolved in water or warm milk. I find that crushing and making a thick paste of saffron with a little water or milk draws more flavour, fragrance and colour out of the saffron.

Salt

Salt flakes, pink salt or any other gourmet salt is not recommended for any recipe. If possible, buy cooking salt from an Indian grocer. Though I have left the amount of seasoning up to the cook, I will say that seasoning is hugely important; it sets a restaurant dish apart from a home-cooked dish. The function of seasoning is to bring out the flavour of all the other ingredients.

Turmeric

In Indian cooking we rarely use fresh turmeric. Dried and ground turmeric brings a flavour that is quite different from fresh, hence in the book when I mention turmeric it almost always specifies ground turmeric.

Spices

Warm

Ayurveda categorises all food items according to their effect on the body. Warm spices are those that create warmth in the body. They include mustard, cinnamon, cassia bark, cloves, turmeric, black cardamom, caraway seeds (ajwain), hing, mace, nutmeg, bay leaf, black pepper, dry ginger and nigella seeds.

Cool

Cooler spices include fennel seeds, cardamom, chilli, cumin seeds, coriander seeds and fenugreek seeds.

Popping

Mustard seeds, cumin seeds, fennel seeds, nigella seeds, sesame seeds and fresh curry leaves can all be popped in oil before adding other main ingredients.

Ground

Ground spices such as ground turmeric, chilli, coriander and cumin should be added when the temperature can be easily controlled. It is best to add spices to your dish in one of the following three ways:

1. Fry ginger and garlic paste in oil for a few minutes before adding ground spices to avoid burning them.

2. Mix your ground spices together with a little water to make a paste, then add to warm or hot oil. Again, they should not burn.

3. Prepare a tadka (see method, page 53) by heating a small amount of oil in a pot or vaghariyu. Once any popping or whole spices have been added, add your ground spices, stir once, then immediately pour the tadka over dal or other prepared dishes. Just make sure your spices are only fried in the hot oil for a couple of seconds.

More delicate ground spices, such as ground ginger, pomegranate, dried mango, mace and nutmeg, should be added later in the cooking process, as they cannot be fried in hot oil, even if first added to water.

Whole

Whole spices, like green cardamom, black cardamom, cassia bark, fennel seeds, cloves, bay leaves, star anise and fenugreek seeds, are all roasted in warm to slightly hot oil before ingredients like onion, ginger or garlic are added. They cannot be added halfway through the preparation. This rule is an exception to the Wazwan cooking of Kashmir where spices are added halfway through.

Use sparingly

Cloves, bay leaves, turmeric, hing, star anise, black cardamom, mustard, mace and nutmeg can all easily overpower a dish and unbalance the flavours. It is recommended to use these more sparingly than other spices. Adding too much can create an irreversible effect.

Meal suggestions

Menu 1

91   Kozhi porichathu

100   Pathiri

Menu 2

45   Baingan sabji

229   Bhatura

186   Heirloom radish pickle

Menu 3

190   Marron head rassam

51   Appam

Menu 4

88   Patrani machi

196   Mango chutney with cinnamon myrtle

       side of rice

195   Lemon myrtle nankhatai

Menu 5

235   Yuzu lassi

159   Aloo paratha

156   Gobi achar

Menu 6

98   Chilli pork

84   Potol dolma

       side of rice

Menu 7

163   Chicken pepper fry

167   Poee

230   Blood orange, quince and riberry pudding with strawberry gum custard

Menu 8

197   Truffled dum aloo

229   Bhatura

Feasts

About the author

Born in Ahmedabad, India, to a Gujarati Patel family, Helly Raichura grew up in India. In her early twenties, she moved to Melbourne, Australia, for university, graduating with a degree in international business and human resource management. She met her husband in Melbourne and has now called the city home for more than a decade.

After graduating, Helly worked in human resources for a few years as she settled into the Australian way of life. During this time, food and cooking provided a refuge whenever she missed her home and culture. Food became a medium of expression for her to educate people and preserve her roots. In 2018, while still working in corporate human resources, Helly opened her home for supper clubs, inviting Melburnians to taste her heritage through regional Indian cooking. She named her supper club Enter Via Laundry, as guests entered the dining area through her laundry.

After gaining much popularity in the Melbourne food scene, Helly started cooking at pop-ups across Melbourne in 2020. Her first restaurant, Enter Via Laundry, opened in Carlton in 2022. The menus at Enter Via Laundry are informed by Helly's travels through India and her in-depth research into and understanding of the history and diversity of Indian cuisine and culture. She incorporates seasonal and Australian native produce on her menu as a way to connect with and pay respect to the land where she cooks and to honour the local produce. In doing so, she keeps the core Indian food philosophy – use seasonal and local produce – alive on her menus.

Acknowledgements

I acknowledge the Wurundjeri people of the Kulin Nation as the Traditional Custodians of our land. I also recognise all Traditional Owners throughout Australia and honour their ongoing connection to land, water and culture. Our respects go to Indigenous Elders past, present and emerging.

This book would not have been possible without the support of my husband, Vishal Raichura, who gives me the strength to keep going, focus on what matters, stay away from unnecessary distractions, forgive often and love more. Thank you, Vishal, for the way of life you believe in that I am part of with you, for all the times when I have been away and you have looked after the family, for the days when I was not present and you brought me back and held me close. You are part of the way I live and think, and so you are very much part of this book.

My mother and father, Preeti and Jignesh Patel: how can I ever thank you enough for your selfless support? You have believed in me, dreamed big for me and been ahead of your time in the way you raised us. Thank you for teaching us to ask the right questions and for sowing the seeds of values and ethics that are now part of everything we do.

Thank you to Hardie Grant for the incredible and tireless work put in by the team. Pam Brewster for believing in this book and finding solutions to hurdles thrown at us. Andrea O'Connor and Claire Davis for keeping us all in check to meet deadlines. Kristin Thomas for a beautiful design that I absolutely cherish. Shivani Prabhu for making this book read the way it reads.

Thank you to all the people who opened their homes, kitchens, restaurants and eateries during my travels in India, who shared their knowledge, heritage, ingredients, stories and passion for food. My journey to learn and explore would not have been possible without you.

Baa, who we lost during the process of making this book, how I wish I could have given it to you as a present. You were the only cook I ever wanted to impress with my work. You inspired me in many ways. I miss you, Baa.

And finally to my motherland, Bharat: no matter where I live you are always beating in my heart. For me, your story of being in this world is the greatest of all. Like a child looking at her mother with love and amazement, I will always look at you to be mesmerised, learn and discover more.

Index

Published in 2025 by Hardie Grant Books,
an imprint of Hardie Grant Publishing

Hardie Grant Books (Melbourne)
Wurundjeri Country
Building 1, 658 Church Street
Richmond, Victoria 3121

Hardie Grant North America
2912 Telegraph Ave
Berkeley, California 94705

hardiegrant.com/books

A catalogue record for this book is available from the National Library of Australia

The Food of Bharat
ISBN 978 1 74379 879 9
ISBN 978 1 76144 019 9 (ebook)

10 9 8 7 6 5 4 3 2 1

Publishing Director: Pam Brewster
Commissioning Editor: Rushani Epa
Head of Editorial: Jasmin Chua
Project Editors: Antonietta Melideo, Claire Davis
Editor: Andrea O'Connor
Designer: Kristin Thomas
Typesetter: Sarah Mawer
Food photography: Jana Langhorst
Location photography: Brett Cole
Stylist: Deborah Kaloper
Head of Production: Todd Rechner
Production Controller: Jessica Harvie

Colour reproduction by Splitting Image Colour Studio
Printed in China by Leo Paper Products LTD.